Endorsements

"Wow, if you are looking for a book to help you start, scale, maximize, or run your business more effectively, this book is for you! Turning Ideas into Impact is truly a treasure trove of valuable golden nuggets of wisdom, practical advice, and sheer relevant brilliance! Each author does a wonderful job of bringing their A game. They share stories, examples, and steps that will help you better yourself, your team, and your business. I can't wait to share this book with my friends and associates because it really does have something for everyone and meets them wherever they may be on their path."

—Steve Rodgers
CEO/President of Alchemy Advisors and former CEO of a Warren Buffet Company

"If you're looking for a book loaded with useful advice and strategies from highly successful, in-demand consultants who have solid track records growing companies and building leaders, this is it."

—Lisa Orrell, CPC
The Personal Development Pro
Keynote Speaker, Author, Leadership and Life Coach, Thought Leader

"Turning Ideas into Impact packs a powerful wallop with its brilliance! Sixteen battle-tested Silicon Valley consultants deliver over 150 Ahas with practical tips designed to maximize your success and help you avoid missteps. The power behind this book is in its diversity of authors, viewpoints, and ideas. Get this book now if you want to succeed faster, bigger, and bolder!"

—Bill Jensen
Author of bestsellers *Simplicity, Disrupt,* and *The Courage Within Us*

"The authors of this excellent book have written some great insights on culture, innovation, and agility and how using principles of aligning around common goals, acting quickly, and adjusting often can reap genuine business benefits. Their wealth of experience shines through in every chapter."

—Mike Stockley
Banking Executive

Turning Ideas Into Impact

Insights from 16 Silicon Valley Consultants

Russell Brand, Hong Nguyen-Phuong, Kimberly Wiefling, Mitchell Levy

An Actionable Business Journal

E-mail: info@thinkaha.com
20660 Stevens Creek Blvd., Suite 210
Cupertino, CA 95014

Copyright © 2020, Russel Brand, Hong Nguyen-Phuong, Kimberly Wiefling, Mitchell Levy

All rights reserved. No part of this book shall be reproduced, stored in a retrieval system, or transmitted by any means other than through the AHAthat platform or with the same attribution shown in AHAthat without written permission from the publisher.

Please go to
http://aha.pub/IdeasIntoImpact
to read this AHAbook and to share the
individual AHAmessages that resonate with you.

Published by THiNKaha®
20660 Stevens Creek Blvd., Suite 210,
Cupertino, CA 95014
https://thinkaha.com
E-mail: info@thinkaha.com

First Printing: February 2020
Hardcover ISBN: 978-1-61699-345-0   1-61699-345-6
Paperback ISBN: 978-1-61699-344-3   1-61699-344-8
eBook ISBN: 978-1-61699-343-6   1-61699-343-X
Place of Publication: Silicon Valley, California, USA
Paperback Library of Congress Number: 2019917324

Trademarks

All terms mentioned in this book that are known to be trademarks or service marks have been appropriately capitalized. Neither THiNKaha, nor any of its imprints, can attest to the accuracy of this information. Use of a term in this book should not be regarded as affecting the validity of any trademark or service mark.

Warning and Disclaimer

Every effort has been made to make this book as complete and as accurate as possible. The information provided is on an "as is" basis. The author(s), publisher, and their agents assume no responsibility for errors or omissions. Nor do they assume liability or responsibility to any person or entity with respect to any loss or damages arising from the use of information contained herein.

Dedication

This book is dedicated to the spirit of Silicon Valley, where failures are called "prototypes," the "impossible" is merely difficult, and dreams become reality.

Acknowledgements

There's a famous African saying: "If you want to go fast, go alone. If you want to go far, go together." This book exists only because of the contributions of sixteen authors who came together to turn this idea into reality, as well as the commitment of many others who supported us on this journey.

Thank you to the authors for their thoughtful contributions and responses to endless requests for their inputs on the many decisions that must be made to create a book such as this. Our executive editor, Kimberly Wiefling (who frequently reminded us that while the book content was non-fiction, the milestone dates were *absolutely* fiction), was assisted by her secret weapon and editor extraordinaire, DeAnna Burghardt. Our publisher, Mitchell Levy, inspired us to take on this challenge, and we heartily appreciate him and his talented team members (especially Jenilee Manti) who made that vision a reality.

Finally, we'd like to thank all our colleagues, clients, customers, and co-conspirators who've helped us learn and grow over the years. Together, they have made the insights contained within this book possible and the impact much more powerful than anything we could have created alone.

Thank you all! - The Authors

How to Read a THiNKaha® Book
A Note from the Authors

The AHAthat/THiNKaha series is the CliffsNotes of the 21st century. These books are contextual in nature. Although the actual words won't change, their meaning will every time you read one as your context will change. Be ready, you will experience your own AHA moments as you read the AHA messages™ in this book. They are designed to be stand-alone actionable messages that will help you think about a project you're working on, an event, a sales deal, a personal issue, etc., differently. As you read this book, please think about the following:

1. It should only take 15–20 minutes to read this book the first time out. When you're reading, write in the underlined area one to three action items that resonate with you.
2. Mark your calendar to re-read this book again in 30 days.
3. Repeat step #1 and mark one to three more AHA messages that resonate. They will most likely be different than the first time. BTW: this is also a great time to reflect on the AHA messages that resonated with you during your last reading.

After reading a THiNKaha book, marking your AHA messages, re-reading it, and marking more AHA messages, you'll begin to see how these books contextually apply to you. AHAthat/THiNKaha books advocate for continuous, lifelong learning. They will help you transform your AHAs into actionable items with tangible results until you no longer have to say AHA to these moments—they'll become part of your daily practice as you continue to grow and learn.

KEEP GROWING & KEEP GOING! - The Authors

Contents

Endorsements	1
Dedication	5
Acknowledgements	6
Executive Editor—Kimberly Wiefling	13
A Poem from Stuart Levine in Honor of This Book	15
Introduction	17

Section I
Being a Consultant, Silicon Valley Style — 19

    Chapter 1
    The Dozen Heroic Secrets of Getting Consulting Clients
    —Russell L. Brand — 21

    Chapter 2
    Credibility: The Key to a Profitable Business
    —Mitchell Levy — 35

    Chapter 3
    Build Just Enough Structure to Help Your Clients
    and Grow Your Business—Carole Amos — 45

Section 2
Methodology Matters in Silicon Valley — 53

    Chapter 4
    21st-Century Business Survival Requires Agile Everything!
    —Hong Nguyen-Phuong — 55

Chapter 5
How Do You Measure Business Success?
—Ellen Grace Henson — 67

Chapter 6
Great Leaders STOP Fads and Pivot, Disrupt, and Transform:
Abandon These Three Fads—Marcia Daszko — 79

Chapter 7
A People-Centered, Value-Focused Approach to Innovation
Management for 21st-Century Organizations—Oliver Yu — 91

Section 3
The Human Side of Silicon Valley — 99

Chapter 8
When the Concern Is Technology,
People Make the Difference—Susan G. Schwartz — 101

Chapter 9
Disrupting Workplace Biases—Matthew Cahill — 111

Chapter 10
For Better Results, Ask Better Questions—Camille Smith — 123

Chapter 11
The Yin and Yang of a Business Transformation:
Culture and Strategic Vision— Amit Patel — 133

Chapter 12
The Right Questions to Ask Yourself When Launching
a New Startup Business—Tom Okada — 145

Chapter 13
Sail to Career Success through Servant Leadership
—Patricia Corcoran — 153

Section 4
Silicon Valley All Over Planet Earth — 161

Chapter 14
The Global Epidemic of Disengaged Employees & Dysfunctional Organizations—Kimberly Wiefling — 163

Chapter 15
Working with Agility: How Executive Leaders Can Spread Silicon Valley Magic—Annie Sheehan — 177

Chapter 16
Leading from Any Chair and Virtually Anywhere! —Jeff Richardson — 187

Appendix — 195

Poet Laureate Stewart Levine's Bio — 198

More About the Executive Editor — 199

Executive Editor — Kimberly Wiefling

Kimberly Wiefling[1] has been consulting in Silicon Valley and globally for the past twenty years through Wiefling Consulting[2] and more recently with her team at Silicon Valley Alliances[3]. A scientist by education, Kimberly has an MS in physics and a BS in chemistry and physics. She worked in HP's analytical products group for nearly ten years, supporting complex systems involving hardware, software, high vacuum, high pressures, gases, liquids, and chemistry, called GCMS/LCMS (mass spectrometers). Her roles included customer service engineering, manufacturing engineering, R&D product development program management, and quality engineering. Kimberly earned her certificate in program and project management through UC Santa Cruz—Silicon Valley, where she then taught program and project management for six years. After more than 100 business trips to Japan and elsewhere in the past decade, she's delighted to now be working closer to home most of the time—driving to work instead of flying!

Kimberly is the executive editor of five books in her "Scrappy About" (https://www.amazon.com/Kimberly-Wiefling/e/B002GWKPOG) series and the author of "Scrappy Project Management", as well as several THiNKaha books.

---

[1] https://kimberlywiefling.com/
[2] https://www.wiefling.com/
[3] https://www.siliconvalleyalliances.com/

This poem was written especially for this book by SV Consultants Poet Laureate Stewart Levine.

Integrity

Congruent within congruent without
Congruent presence toes to shout
Congruent in gait and voice
How it is never a choice

Not about image strategic vision
Just how you live clarity precision
End of day you finish labor
Lie down rest with warmth to savor

You are who you are do what you say
Your word a bond to honor each day
Called upon you counsel the poor
Nurture who walks through your door

Living from inside out
Heart your guide no twist or shout
Whatever your truth and belief
Oath guides action brings relief

Not about mercenary ambition
Focused dedication to your mission
When nearing end look back reflect
Lived your dream no need repent

Introduction

Silicon Valley is recognized globally as a hotbed of innovation and entrepreneurship. It's the birthplace of world-famous companies like Apple, Google, and Facebook and home to some of the legends of NASA at the Ames Research Center.

A major contributor to the Silicon Valley phenomenon is our diversity. Half of us don't speak English at home. And our diversity goes far beyond ethnicity. A wide variety of perspectives, thinking styles, and work approaches also contribute to the magic of Silicon Valley, creating breakthroughs that have disrupted business models (AirBnB and Lyft) and even shifted our perception of the future of meat (the "Impossible Burger").

We're also one of the most educated regions in the US—nearly half of us graduated college, and about a fifth have earned graduate degrees. Businesses here are filled with smart, well-educated, experienced people. But like all organizations made up of human beings, we are subject to the same pitfalls that threaten companies everywhere.

Many businesses that were successful 100 years ago no longer exist. Trapped by their own success they gradually learned to reduce risk and avoid failure at all costs, and consequently squelched or killed innovation and creativity. This made them vulnerable to competition from new or more aggressive companies with less to lose. Are your greatest contributions and successes behind you or ahead of you? Even brilliant people can underperform—or fail—for entirely predictable (and avoidable!) reasons.

Similar hazards face successful executives, professionals, and leaders of every kind. One danger of success is the increased difficulty of recognizing and adjusting to shifts in the business environment. No one knows this better than the former leaders of Nokia and Kodak, two once-great brands that ignored the timeless wisdom that a peak always conceals a treacherous valley. It can be hard to see new possibilities that will allow future success, especially when it requires letting go of previously effective strategies that served you well. This is where the outside perspective of a consultant can be particularly useful and where this book may offer an alternative to that treacherous valley.

Introduction

Organizations need support to turn their talented employees and potential into real teams with viable strategies that can produce excellent results—preferably by design, not merely by luck. In spite of the myth of the "lone genius," breakthroughs in Silicon Valley emerge from teamwork. Very little happens without the support of others, whether team members, advisors, mentors, investors, coaches—or consultants.

This book is a peek into the world of Silicon Valley consultants. The diversity of this community makes their observations relevant globally. Whether you want to benefit from their experience or be a consultant yourself, you'll discover valuable insights, practical approaches, and effective methodologies that can benefit you and your organization.

If you'd like to double your chances of success, increase revenues and profits, and fail—if you *do* fail—for new and more exciting reasons, you will benefit from the wisdom shared in this book. Mine these insights, garnered from hundreds of years of experience fighting the real-world dragons of organizational culture and corporate malaise. Apply them to optimize your results and accelerate growth. There are treasures here that can benefit every business, from one-person firms to global giants.

"An open-minded and diverse population that readily shares information, encourages experimentation, accepts failure and dispenses with formality and hierarchy is what makes Silicon Valley the successful hub that it is."
—Vivek Wadhwa

Section I

Being a Consultant, Silicon Valley Style

Chapter I

The Dozen Heroic Secrets of Getting Consulting Clients

Author: Russell L. Brand

Russell Brand has founded three successful companies and advised and made angel investments in hundreds more. His current focus is on crafting investor and customer stories to enable early stage companies to have their offerings valued and appreciated.

Russell offers strategic advising to companies of all sizes and shapes. He has done noted work in open source adoption, artificial intelligence-aided software engineers, and computer security and has sold and been awarded six patents in the organization of computer storage. Several of his projects have individually resulted in tens to hundreds of millions of dollars in savings to US taxpayers. He has been active in several angel investment groups, including Keiretsu Forum and MIT Angels.

Russell received his masters from University of California, Berkeley, and his bachelor's degree from MIT, where he was a member of Tau Beta Pi and an officer of Eta Kappa Nu.

Email: brand@QuietCandor.com
Website: http://www.QuietCandor.com/
LinkedIn: https://www.linkedin.com/in/russell-brand/

The Dozen Heroic Secrets of Getting Consulting Clients

Introduction
It is hard to get customers and hard to keep them, much harder than it should be. There are a few small, simple, but vitally important secrets to getting customers for a consulting business. They are not taught, as far as I know, in any class nor have they ever been collected together in one place. These secrets are just as vital for salespeople, teachers, advocates, and leaders of all kinds as they are for consultants.

By way of an example, I will speak here of building a bridge over a raging river. It's easier to use a concrete (no pun intended) example than to draw on actual cases that would require a detailed explanation of the task.

Secret 1: Start with the Problem
Do not say, "I build bridges." That is a solution. Start instead with the problem—the pain for which your solution is the painkiller—which is that people can't quickly, easily, and safely get to the places, people, organizations, and other resources on the other side of a raging river.

Secret 2: You Are a Hero
When you build that metaphorical bridge, you are keeping people alive who would have wrongly thought they could just walk or swim across that raging river. They may never know that you and your "bridge" saved them.

That doesn't make you any less of a hero.

Children will get educations. Businesses will start and succeed. People will form friendships and romances, have children, and live happily ever after. Without your bridge, they would not have been able to do those things. They may never think about your bridge or about you, but you are a hero nonetheless.

No matter what happens with any particular project or bid, never forget that you are a hero. A hero who creates great value.

Secret 3: The Problem Is Valuable

The problem that your prospective client is working on is more important than most people realize—more important than even the prospect realizes. Our "bridge" client probably is thinking about the time saved and greater convenience of a potential solution. Maybe they are contemplating improved commerce. Perhaps it's about access to schools.

They probably aren't thinking about the children who won't be orphans, the spouses who won't be widowed, the otherwise lonely people who would never have found one another that are now families living happily ever after.

You deeply appreciate the value of their project. You see it. You see it more clearly than anyone ever has. And because of you, your client better appreciates the project's value and their own potential to become a hero.

Secret 4: Empathy Transforms You from a Hero into a Superhero

Stan Lee, one of my personal heroes, always reminded us that what makes a superhero a superhero is not their superpower, but their super heart. Empathy is understanding your client's situation and caring about their success—*this* is what can elevate you from being a hero to being a superhero!

Empathy enables us to ask better questions. It reduces the risk that you will solve the wrong problem or solve it in a totally unacceptable manner. Solving the wrong problem is surprisingly common.

Empathy will enable the prospective client to trust you. People generally don't hire people they don't trust.

Secret 5: Superheroes Have Nothing to Prove

Superheroes don't need to use confusing jargon to show clients that they know things. Confusing the client and making them feel small won't win you long-term, valuable, loyal clients. Your job is to remind your client of their competence, not to make them feel dumb. When you're a superhero, your clients are brilliant, it's easy to see this, and they want to work with you.

It's not helpful to tell your prospects that they have it all wrong and that you can do better. It is not that the selected siting of their "bridge" sucks or that you can pick a better spot. It's that another site may further their vision.

Each and every word you say is about how to make your client's vision stronger, more real, more high-potential, and most of all, more successful.

As one of the most popular US presidents, Ronald Reagan, once said, "There is no limit to the amount of good you can do if you don't care who gets the credit."

Secret 6: Superheroes Are Always Polite

As a consultant, leader, or superhero, you are always being judged. Courtesy and respect matter. Your behavior matters not only to your clients but also to the receptionist at your client's office, to the service people when you are meeting at a hotel or restaurant, and to everyone you interact with.

Remember that service and support people do important work. It is not just that they make it possible for your work to get done, but they also directly touch the lives of many, many people. Their interactions can have a big impact on the quality of life for the entire ecosystem around them. Your courtesy, patience, and appreciation allow them to better perform this important work.

Secret 7: Even as a Superhero, You Are Not *the* Hero

Your prospective client/customer is the Hero. Even if you are providing a complete solution that solves the entire problem, they are still *the* hero, not you and not your solution. What you provide is a tool, a prop, or an instrumentality that allows your client to achieve the solution, vanquish the evil, save the world (or at least the proverbial princess), and succeed.

Our collective memory from the beginning of time is filled with sages, mentors, and even fairy godmothers. They are not the heroes of the stories. They give the protagonist a wish, a map, or a magic sword—something that allows the hero-to-be to succeed and become the Hero.

Your client/customer becomes the Hero and gets the raise, promotion, or spotlight or appears on the cover of *Time* magazine because of you catalyzing and enabling their success. It is their story, not yours.

Each client is the Hero of their own story.

Secret 8: You Make Things Look Too Easy

Because your heart is pure, your training is good, or your experience is on point, you can complete your part of the project faster and better than your client or their organization. That is why you were chosen.

You may well do in a day or week something that would have taken a large customer team a month or year to complete. But they may overlook that because after you finish your work, there is generally still much to do that will have to be done by others. It is easy for the client to forget the years you saved them and instead, remember only how much time you spent on the work. Your contributions can frequently appear trivial compared to the time and effort required for the remaining work, the work your client must now do.

Before you begin, restate your understanding of the scope of what they would like accomplished.

Ask the client what it would take to achieve this using only their internal resources.

Before you leave, ask the client what was accomplished. Ask the client how much time and effort would have been required for them to achieve this progress on their own. You have created value, and you should be recognized, appreciated, and paid on the basis of that value. You are a hero (though not *the* Hero).

Secret 9: The World Is Full of Flakes

People don't keep commitments. Remind them before they are embarrassingly late, whether that is answering a question, providing a resource, or paying their bills. People don't finish things. Often a 90% completion is worth nothing, the proverbial "bridge to nowhere."

Chapter 1: The Dozen Heroic Secrets of Getting Consulting Clients

Your hard work, even if you have been paid well for it, will often amount to nothing because the client drops the ball. Make sure that this doesn't happen to your projects. Make sure that your contribution isn't lost. Regularly ask about progress.

Secret 11: Details Matter
Attention to details matters. If your spelling, grammar, alignment, or arithmetic is wrong on your websites, handouts, or proposals, why should the client trust your work?

If you are late for a meeting, why should a client trust that your deliverables will be done on time?

Fortunately, since you are a superhero, you immediately noticed that the numbering of this section is wrong, and you were already considering how to send a private note to let us know. (You never would have considered embarrassing us with a public posting—that is more for supervillains!)

Secret 12: Even If You Are a Mere Mortal, Your Work Is Still Important
Any job where you interact with other people is important work. No matter your job description or task goals, because you have a chance to interact with others, you have a chance to influence their lives. A kind word, an empathetic ear, or a compassionate act might not win you a contract, a raise, or a promotion. Avoiding losing your temper, or resisting the urge to feel smart at someone else's expense, might not even be necessary to avoid losing that contract, raise, or promotion. However, that doesn't reduce their importance.

Even if you don't want to be a super*hero* or even just a hero, you can still bring a super*heart* to everything you do.

Secret 13: Value-Creating Projects Tend to Be More Difficult Than They First Appear
There will be setbacks, errors that take time to fix, and false starts.

The fact that something doesn't work the first time is no reason to quit. It's no reason to doubt yourself. It's not an indication that you're not a superhero.

Including extra time and resources in your plan to allow for surprises doesn't make you a coward. It makes you prudent—a prudent superhero your client can rely upon.

Conclusion

- None of this is difficult.
- None of this is surprising.
- It's just small stuff that we don't normally think about.
- It's small stuff that no one teaches us.
- It's small stuff we get right from practice.
- It's small stuff that matters—small stuff with a big impact.

Chapter 1: The Dozen Heroic Secrets of Getting Consulting Clients

1

Showing appreciation is payment without cost.

_____

_____

_____

2

Explaining why something matters should precede understanding how it works.

_____

_____

_____

3

It's harder to be "better than nothing" than it sounds. Many products and services are not. Even some successful products fail this test.

_____

_____

_____

4

Almost everything of importance requires a team. Every team begins with one person who cares.

_____

_____

_____

5

The true value of good notes is most quickly realized by those who fail to take them.

_____

_____

_____

6

Kindness is never wasted.

_____

_____

_____

7

I am grateful to be able to awake asking, "How can I make the lives of those I care about more wonderful?" and have a chance to endeavor to do so.

_____

_____

_____

8

Never underestimate the joy that you bring to those around you when you allow them to help you.

_____

_____

_____

9

Crashing and burning later is almost always more expensive than taking a break now.

_____

_____

_____

10

All work is important work. Whatever the task description, we have the opportunity to practice kindness, compassion & simple courtesy. Alternatively, we can degrade our work into unimportant work. It truly is our choice.

_____

_____

_____

Chapter 2

Credibility: The Key to a Profitable Business

Author: Mitchell Levy

Global Credibility Expert Mitchell Levy is a TEDx speaker and international bestselling author of over 60 books. As The AHA Guy at AHAthat (https://AHAthat.com), he helps extract the genius from your head in a two-to-three-hour interview, so his team can ghostwrite your book, publish it, distribute it, and make you an Amazon bestselling author in four months. He is an accomplished entrepreneur who has created twenty businesses in Silicon Valley, including four publishing companies that have published over 850 books. He's provided strategic consulting to over 100 companies, and he has been chairman of the board of a NASDAQ-listed company. Mitchell has been happily married for thirty years and regularly spends four weeks in Europe with family and friends.

Connect to Mitchell on social media or book time on his calendar by going to https://MitchellLevy360.com.

Email: Mitchell.Levy@THiNKaha.com
Website: https://www.THiNKaha.com/
LinkedIn: https://www.linkedin.com/in/mitchelllevy/

Credibility: The Key to a Profitable Business

Ninety-eight percent of the time, prospects research your product or service on the Internet before they speak to you or your firm. If they are researching you and nine other competitors and then picking three to explore in more detail, how can you be one of those three?

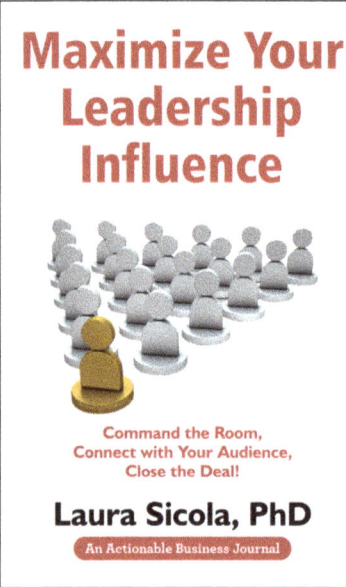

Make sure your online presence screams credibility!
"People have to buy into you first before they buy into your product, service, or idea. #Credibility @LauraSicola" —*Maximize Your Leadership Influence* by Laura Sicola (http://aha.pub/LeadershipInfluenceAmazon)

I've heard many IT professionals make the following statement when including their top three vendors: "You can't go wrong by choosing IBM." What they are really saying is, "If the project goes bad, I won't be fired because IBM has a name that connotes trust, and no one will say, 'Why did you try that other firm?'"

From Dictionary.com: "Credibility is the quality of being trusted and believed in." If you want to make it to the table so you have an opportunity to make a sale, you need to be continually demonstrating your credibility.

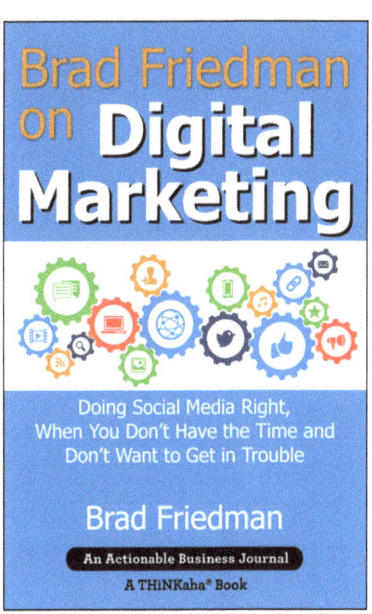

"The #Relationship and the #Sale requires the establishment of #Trust and the building of #Credibility. @TonyAlessandra" —*Tony Alessandra on People Smart in Business* (http://aha.pub/PeopleSmartAmazon)

The TEDx talk I gave focused on one (http://aha.pub/TEDtalk) primary thought: we do business with those we KNOW, LIKE, and TRUST! If that is the case, you need to be known. Once known, you have to be liked and trusted. So, what can you be doing as a company to be trusted and believed in?

"People do biz with people, not businesses. Use your brand's social channels to develop relationships, trust, and credibility. @BradFriedman" —*Brad Friedman on Digital Marketing* (http://aha.pub/DigitalMarketingAmazon)

At this stage of the evaluation process, your prospects are looking at the credibility that the people in your company are demonstrating. How many experts are in your firm, what thought leadership tips are they sharing, what communities are they participating in, what conferences are they speaking at, what webinars are they giving, and what books have they written?

When your prospects are interacting with your employees, how do they feel? Do they feel warm and fuzzy? How can you help your employees generate the quality of being trusted and believed in?

Help them be seen as credible experts!

When you help your employees be seen as experts, you'll experience something beautiful. You'll experience a situation where the sum of the parts is greater than the whole. How can you help your employees demonstrate credibility? Here's a list of things you can encourage them to do:

1. Authoring a book. The best credibility tool on the market today is a book, particularly one that focuses on your CPoP (Customer Point of Pain). Check out https://AHAthat.com/Author to see how your employees can easily write a book, or have us ghostwrite one, where they can be Amazon best-selling authors in four months after spending five-ten hours.
2. Speaking and teaching. Encourage and support your employees to speak at events and teach at local universities, as well as worldwide via online webinars.
3. Getting awards/certifications/certificates. Encourage your employees to get credentialed by getting certificates and certifications. Also, encourage them to apply for awards in their areas of expertise. After receiving these credentials, share on both the corporate's and the employee's social media. When your prospects check out your employees' LinkedIn pages, what do they see?
4. Gathering customer testimonials. For every opportunity where it makes sense, get customer testimonials in written, spoken, and visual modalities to include on your website and in your and your employees' social media.
5. Making a website. Have a compelling website that demonstrates credibility and is continually updated. It doesn't have to be the best thing since sliced bread, but it can't be below average.
6. Utilizing social media. Your social media should educate your prospect base. You should also highlight the accomplishments and expertise of your employees.

These are just a few tools you can use to increase the credibility of your employees and your firm. If you want to continue to expand your customer base, you need to demonstrate the credibility of your organization through your employee base. It's not a difficult process, but it does require that you trust and support your employees, as their success will lead toward your success.

11

Your prospects do business with those they know, like, and trust. When your employees demonstrate their #Credibility, your awareness, likeability, and trust will grow in the marketplace.

_____

_____

_____

12

#Credibility is the quality of being trusted and believed in. Without it, you do not have a business. Having it allows you to be at the table.

_____

_____

_____

Chapter 2: Credibility: The Key to a Profitable Business

13

One key secret to a long-term business is continually working on and sharing your #Credibility with referral partners and clients. What have you done this week?

_____

_____

_____

14

Want prospects to buy into your business? Have them buy into you first. #Credibility

_____

_____

_____

15

Demonstrating #Credibility in your online presence helps you stand out among the competition.

_____

_____

_____

16

For prospects to see your business as credible, your employees need to demonstrate their #Credibility.

_____

_____

_____

17

Having your employees seen as #CredibleExperts generates the trust your prospects need to do business with you.

18

Expand your customer base by demonstrating the #Credibility of your org through your employee base.

19

Your employees' #Credibility and success lead to your success. Are you helping your employees be credible and successful?

_____
_____
_____

20

There are many tools you can deploy to allow your employees to demonstrate their #Credibility. Books are one of the best tools on the market and are extremely easy to create these days.

_____
_____
_____

Chapter 3

Build Just Enough Structure to Help Your Clients and Grow Your Business

Author: Carole Amos

Carole Amos specializes in amping up indirect sales, with expertise in channel marketing and sales operations for software, hardware, and services. She has over 20 years of experience marketing and launching high-tech products and services into the channel in the US and international markets.

Carole is known for establishing and maintaining strong, trusting relationships with business partners by listening to them, understanding their business and their needs, championing them, and creating programs for mutual success.

Born and raised in upstate New York—way upstate—Carole is delighted to have made her way to Silicon Valley to live and work. Her technical mind, once satisfied by earning a degree in electrical engineering and working as a software developer, evolved to her getting an MBA and working in technical marketing. Carole enjoys being outdoors, reveling in the beautiful landscape and weather for a hike, bike ride, or street-side dining. She still believes that libraries are mankind's best invention.

Email: Carole@caroleamos.com
WEBSITE: http://channel-savvy.com
LinkedIn: https://www.linkedin.com/in/carole/

Build Just Enough Structure to Help Your Clients and Grow Your Business

It can be difficult to work on your own consulting business when you're deep into working with your clients. They have a hole to fill or just won the budget to get something done that the current team wasn't able to achieve. Stepping in, seamlessly picking up the threads, and carrying the project forward are what clients are ostensibly paying for. However, if you can think strategically about their business while you're being strategic with your own business, you not only can accomplish your proposed projects but also develop processes for them that will serve as marketing materials for *you*. Here are my key insights.

21

Successful consulting means you must always be networking — even though it's difficult to keep looking for new clients while you're working with existing ones. Network within each client engagement!

22

Tune your marketing so it speaks to your prospective client's pain: What can't they do without you? What are you crucial for — what is the "painkiller"?

23

Capture your learnings and insights as you're networking. Turn them into posts or articles to build up your professional portfolio and credibility.

_____

_____

_____

24

Learning how your work product will flow into your client's processes will help your contributions see the light of day and provide you with another success story.

_____

_____

_____

25

Avoid providing custom work for free in the hopes that you will be hired. What people pay for, they value. If they offer value in return for your contributions, they will likely be a good client.

_____

_____

_____

26

Know your own values. Even if the gig is tempting, if you know the prospective client has different values than you, don't take it. That's a dealbreaker.

_____

_____

_____

27

Your clients are likely not familiar with your specialty. Having materials that explain why you need to do certain things and the process that you use will give them a reference point and make it easier for you to persuade them of your value.

_____

_____

28

Keep a daily log of what you've done for each client. This will provide details for your invoices, supporting information if you need to remind them of all you've done, and valuable input for your marketing materials.

_____

_____

29

Help your client be strategic. Beyond what they hired you to do, occasionally talk with them about how their work fits into the "big picture" and how they are providing what their boss needs.

30

Provide a framework for every project that you do. Share insights into your process with your client, and expose assumptions early on to ensure smooth delivery and ideally, follow-up work.

Section 2

Methodology Matters in Silicon Valley

Chapter 4

21st-Century Business Survival Requires Agile Everything!

Author: Hong Nguyen-Phuong

Hong Nguyen-Phuong challenges and inspires teams to fully engage, lead, and innovate. He co-founded Hotaru Media and is a member of Silicon Valley Alliances. Hong studied engineering at MIT, computer science at Boston University, and general management at Harvard Business School. He is committed to learning constantly in interactions with stakeholders and teams to bring innovation and value to market. His 2019 engagements brought to market a food logistics platform and a block-chained communications platform. Hong is certified in project management, Scrum, and scaled agile. Active in local communities, he is most proud of being awarded Individual Member of the Year by the Silicon Valley Central Chamber of Commerce.

Email: hong.nguyenp@gmail.com
Website: https://siliconvalleyalliances.com/
LinkedIn: https://www.linkedin.com/in/hongnguyenp/

Chapter 4: 21st-Century Business Survival Requires Agile Everything!

21st-Century Business Survival Requires Agile Everything!

We are one-fifth of the way into the 21st century, and businesses do not lack new markets to pursue nor flexible resources and technology to leverage. Opportunities are more plentiful than ever *if* you can master the art of being agile in this rapidly changing global business ecosystem. When Microsoft co-founder Bill Gates addressed Harvard students in 2018, he said that they were more fortunate to be a Harvard student than when he had started in 1973, because today, they can study exciting new innovations and solve big, complex problems. This is truly a time of global opportunity for anyone willing to seize the tremendous possibilities!

- While the populations of advanced countries are shifting toward elderly and retiring segments, global human population overall increases by over 80 million each year. Countries such as Nigeria, India, Mexico, and Brazil have younger populations, while the UK, Spain, Germany, and Japan are at the other end of the spectrum.
- Any company can now easily access fully functional offices on a month-to-month rental basis, including remote office space in major cities around the world. Co-working spaces are on the rise, and nearly 90% of people who took advantage of this option reported that they were happier after joining a coworking space (http://ergonomictrends.com/coworking-space-statistics/).
- Today, software permeates products and services in every industry sector. The open source software model is now in its third generation, leveraging entire communities of developers and their code worldwide. This makes it ever faster, easier, and less expensive for companies to experiment, develop, test, deploy, and market their software (https://techcrunch.com/2019/01/12/how-open-source-software-took-over-the-world/).
- For electronic hardware, the trend is toward increased outsourcing, from contract manufacturers to original design manufacturers. Besides operating factories with low-cost labor and transportation, the latter also create their own intellectual property and proactively pursue their own patents, benefitting both clients and buyers. Independent compliance testing labs cater to businesses of all sizes, helping them meet global industry and military standards.

With three billion smartphone users worldwide, connecting with consumers has become much more direct. Early pilot users can directly reach your technical experts. And after your product has scaled, they can just as easily reach your remote call center (https://newzoo.com/insights/trend-reports/newzoo-global-mobile-market-report-2018-light-version/).

Regarding customer support, blockchain and "crypto" businesses now practice open communication with dozens to hundreds of thousands on platforms like Telegram or WeChat.

For many companies vying for a global footprint, such developments will continue to exacerbate two profound and widespread changes in product development of the past decade: the dramatic shrinkage of product lifespan and the need for enterprise agility to address proliferating complexities. What kind of complexity? Complexity in deciding what to make and how to make it. Across industry sectors, 50 percent of company revenues annually are now derived from products launched within the past three years. Within technology industries, two-year product and service lifecycles have become the norm. Better coordination across the entire supply chain has become an essential requirement for success, along with accurate demand planning and forecasting.

Companies that are unable to step up to sufficient levels of nimbleness risk launching goods and services shunned by users and quickly displaced by competitors. Witness the rapid demise of Nokia from a dominant position in its industry. In 2010, Nokia held a staggering 53% market share. Within five years, that dropped to nearly zero, while during this exact timeframe, Apple and Samsung grew to be wildly successful in the very same market space!

In a recent update about the mobile phone industry, market leaders Samsung and Apple faltered this past year while Huawei surged 50%, shipping 59 million units. Meanwhile Vivo grew 24% by selling low-end phones in India. In hindsight, Nokia's demise was indeed needlessly premature.

The process of creating new products that were unimaginable not long ago involves specialists and cross-functional teams, as well as supply chain partners outside of

Chapter 4: 21st-Century Business Survival Requires Agile Everything!

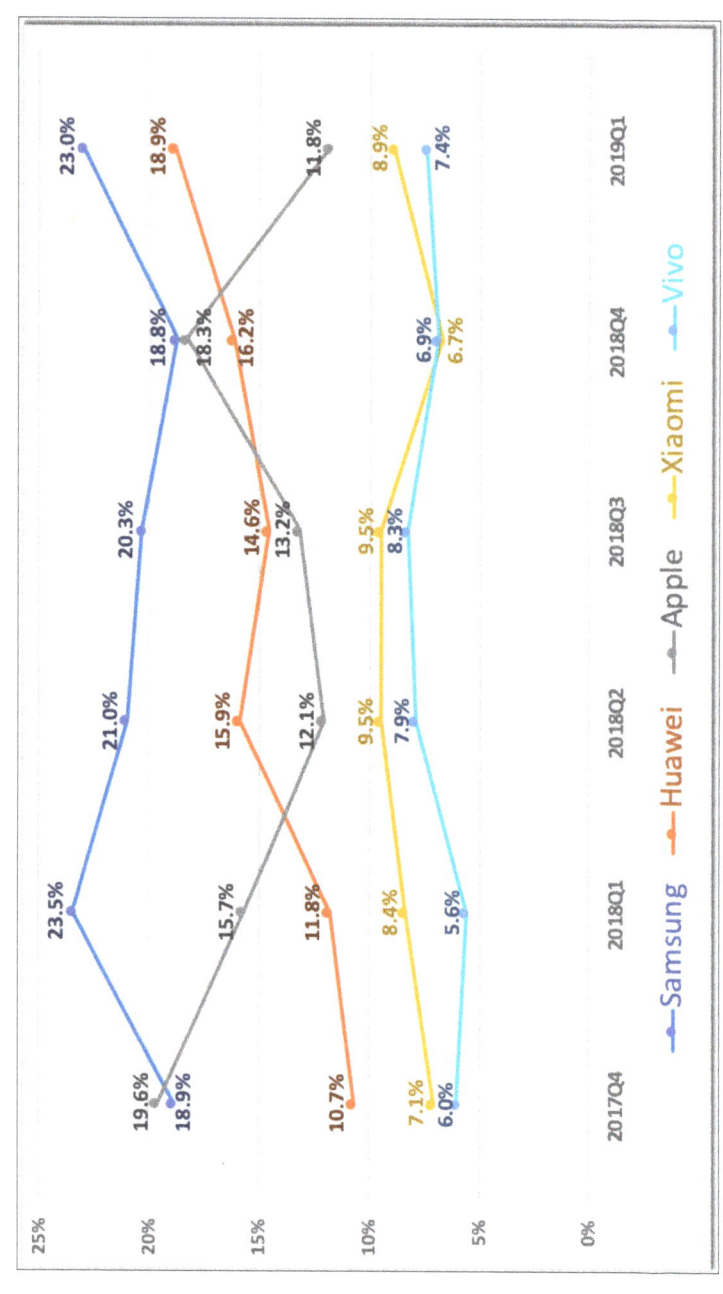

the organization. Excellence is measured by the launch of successful products and services that spark excitement with customers, employees, and investors. In order for employees to exercise the imagination required to generate this kind of innovation, they need to trust that executives are committed to long-term success. Individuals need to trust that their team members' commitment can be counted on—that they will deliver as promised and demonstrate that commitment and follow-through at every phase and with every iteration.

With the extreme demand of personal time that this environment requires, one commodity has become much more scarce: the selective attention of employees and consumers. To endure and thrive, leaders and companies must enthusiastically embrace agile values, agile principles, and an agile mindset, as well as agile practices. In the rush to "do agile" (meaning to implement the famous agile methodology that has become so popular) and reap the anticipated benefits, many obsess about less vital matters, such as instituting sprints, publishing a product backlog, or deciding between software tools such as Jira or Rally. What is far more fundamental and beneficial to success is that everyone understands and completely buys into agile values such as: transparency, inspection, adaptation, alignment, and built-in quality. (Raise your hand if you truly believe quality can be inspected-in!) In order to be truly agile, they must learn what experienced agile practitioners have time and again relied upon: enduring principles such as minimizing work-in-progress and decentralizing frequent and urgent decisions.

Agile means to be able to move quickly and easily. Agile teams find ways to remain fresh, inspired, and committed. Agile leaders know how to rally their teams in support of their organization's purpose, mission, and vision, as well as encouraging them to remain adaptable in the face of inevitable change. Agile *doesn't* mean a lack of long-term thinking or detailed planning. At Silicon Valley Alliances, we constantly remind our clients to clarify their Big Why and What and then let them figure out the Big How. Often, just a few minutes of planning can dramatically improve the chances of success and the quality of the final outcome. When planning is agile and adaptable, re-planning can be done just as swiftly, enabling a strong team to navigate even the most rapidly changing environment. That's agile. Agile teams use just enough planning to optimize results, then experiment, prototype, test, learn, and adapt. The recipe for survival for 21st-century businesses? Agile everything!

31

Traditional consumer markets are aging and shrinking, but elsewhere younger new markets are growing. Look and you will find!

32

It is getting easier, cheaper, and faster to develop products and services with technology components. Businesses will scale faster too!

33

Widespread global adoption of smartphones has made it easier to connect directly with consumers worldwide.

34

One paradox for many global companies is that products are becoming more complex to develop but have a shorter lifespan.

35

Even companies with staggering market dominance can irreversibly fall by the wayside in just a few years, while new players surge to the top.

36

Teams fail without trust, and trust must be earned by everyone, every day, through repeated commitment, consistency, and follow-through.

37

Everyone in the organization must understand and completely buy into the values of transparency, inspection, adaptation, alignment, and built-in quality.

_____

_____

_____

38

Certain principles for success are enduring, such as minimizing work-in-progress and decentralizing frequent and urgent decisions.

_____

_____

_____

39

Leaders must check in constantly with their teams so they remain strong, fresh, inspired, and committed to "success." The culture of continuous learning needs constant nurturing.

_____

_____

_____

40

One of the highest responsibilities of a leader is to rally their teams to support their organization's mission and vision. Communicate and clarify the Big WHY and WHAT, and then let them figure out the Big HOW.

_____

_____

_____

Chapter 5

How Do You Measure Business Success?

Author: Ellen Grace Henson

Ellen Grace Henson helps business leaders and teams engage in strategic conversations regarding what is at the core of their organization: their customers. With experience in multiple markets and technologies, Ellen Grace brings a unique combination of analysis and creativity to business and product strategy, market and customer insight, and product-delivery process design. She has particular expertise in aligning cross-functional teams to deliver high levels of customer satisfaction and strong business results.

Alignment ThinkTanks™, a series of highly adaptable workshops, provide opportunities for teams to co-create alignment and engagement, starting with simple conversations and growing toward an environment where people, programs, processes, products, and services thrive through achievement of customer-centric goals.

Email: egh@mktgmech.com
Website: http://www.mktgmech.com/
LinkedIn: https://www.linkedin.com/in/ellengracehenson/

How Do You Measure Business Success?

Regardless of which key metrics you use for insights into business performance, it's important to understand what actions and situations influence those metrics. Internal alignment and employee engagement are two factors with huge impact on business results.

Some months ago, I had the opportunity to talk with Nicole La, executive vice president at TEECOM, a private company that delivers technology solutions across enterprises in partnership with architects, building owners, developers, and contractors. A 2017 *San Francisco Business Times* "Fast 100" designee, TEECOM starts driving customer-centric alignment the moment they bring on new employees. Employee onboarding includes a strong focus on the company brand promise, value proposition, and customer needs. Thereafter, team members participate in customer journey mapping and cross-functional role-playing so the firm can continuously improve its culture and the value offered to their clients. As TEECOM continues with its rapid growth, they are definitely a company to watch.

The Impact of Engagement
Employee engagement is a positive motivational connection that an employee feels with their organization, influencing them to apply discretionary effort to their work. Engagement has been shown in numerous studies to be linked to positive organizational and employee outcomes. High engagement is associated with increased profitability, sales growth, and employee retention, as well as improved customer satisfaction and loyalty. The impact of high and low engagement is illustrated in the graph below, which was created by marketing mechanics from multi-study data presented in "CFO Advisory: Employee Engagement Impacts Financial Outcomes and Business Risk" by Gartner, Inc., published March 13, 2013.

Turning Ideas Into Impact

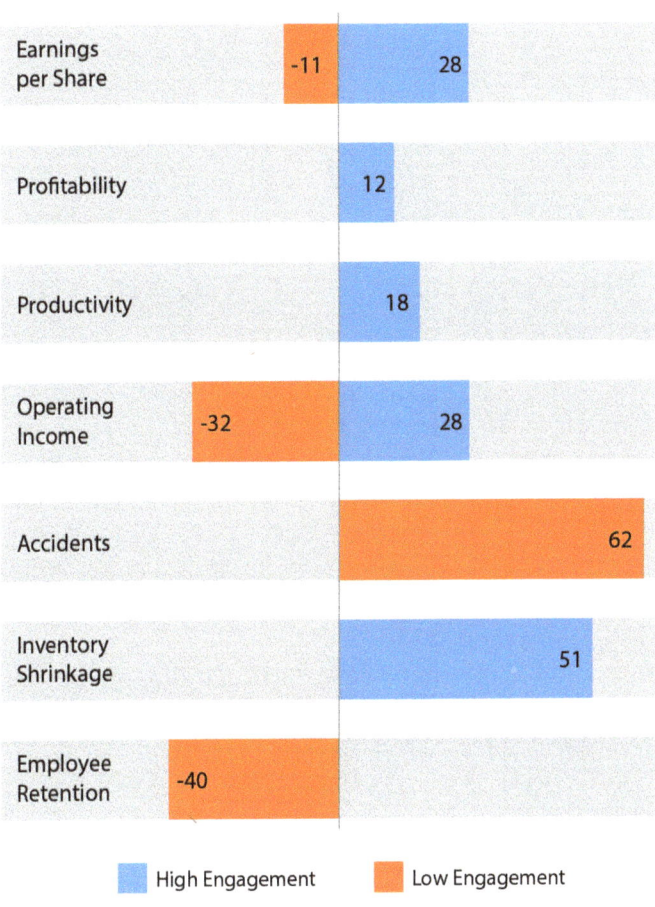

Graphic created by Marketing Mechanics from multi-study data present in "CFO Advisory: Employee Engagement Impacts Financial Outcomes and Business Risk" Gartner, Inc., published March 13, 2013.

This makes sense, of course. People who feel unengaged—disconnected from or disenchanted by their work environment—aren't likely operating at a high level of performance. From an alignment point of view, you might have great enthusiasm and energy from people and teams who are all running in different directions, gaining little in the way of business momentum.

What Does True Alignment Look Like?
Alignment can be defined as the degree to which employees value and believe in the vision, mission, and goals of their organization. When employees value and believe in organizational goals and see how their work contributes to their company's values, they experience a greater sense of purpose in their work. Alignment can drive engagement, amplifying positive business results.

A Shared Understanding of the Customer
A shared understanding of who the customer is and the metrics associated with customer satisfaction and success present the most natural and neutral focus for alignment—in part because the customer is a human face to the business. This human face can be a relatable focus for the work that each and every employee does. TEECOM, with their customer-focused new employee on-boarding, and a continuing focus on the customer, reaps the benefits of alignment and engagement for the organization and its employees, customers, and partners.

Mergers and Acquisitions Pose Particular Alignment Challenges
Depending on whose research you look at, mergers have a failure rate of anywhere between 50 and 90 percent. Cultural integration issues are frequently cited as a top reason that mergers fail. Alignment and engagement initiatives can be important in overcoming cultural challenges, and involving employees in the overall merger process helps assure that they are on board and contributing to progress for the execution phase. Cross-functional teams representing the pre-merger entities provide valuable insights into which practices from each can combine into a stronger, more successful post-merger organization.

Alignment and Engagement Deliver Business Results
Regardless of your organization's size or stage of growth, increasing alignment and employee engagement will have an impact on both top line and bottom line metrics. Here are suggestions on how to support alignment and engagement across your organization:

- Document company goals.
- Define target customers and get to know them in detail.
- Ensure that all employees are familiar with your vision, mission, and goals; who your customers are; and what customers need, want, and are willing to pay for.
  - o Remember that your customers might have different roles as well: buyer, influencer, end user, etc.
- Provide support for individuals and cross-functional teams to engage and collaborate on delivering true value to your customers.

41

Teams are more effective when they are aligned and engaged around shared purpose and goals. #CustomerNeeds are a natural and neutral source of shared purpose and goals.

_____

_____

_____

42

Customers pay for value. It takes aligned and engaged teams to deliver optimal value to customers at every interaction throughout all phases and aspects of the relationship.

_____

_____

_____

43

To answer this question, "Is #ShareholderValue more important than #CustomerSatisfaction?", ask this question: "Without satisfied and loyal customers, what sustainable value is there for shareholders?"

_____

_____

_____

44

Business leaders and teams need to engage in strategic conversations around what is at the center of their company—the customer!

_____

_____

_____

45

To gain #insight into what your customers need, want, and are willing to pay for, follow this 80/20 rule: 20% of the time ask open-ended questions, 80% of the time observe and listen.

46

#Alignment and #EmployeeEngagement around a shared understanding of the #Customer can be a corporate superpower — driving higher profits, #CustomerSatisfaction, and #EmployeeRetention.

47

If a customer asks whether your solution does X, don't say yes or no. Instead, ask them why X would be valuable to them. Focus less on specific features and more on understanding what they are trying to achieve.

48

Ask (in a conversational, not challenging way) five people within your company, "Who is our customer?" If you get more than one answer, the individuals and teams are not aligned.

49

Make time to sit down with people from other parts of your organization and discuss how your teams might #Collaborate more effectively on delivering value to your #Customers.

50

A shared understanding of what customers need, want, and will pay for can ignite insight and #Innovation across an organization.

_____

_____

_____

P!VOT

How Leaders Beat

D!SRUPT

the Odds and Survive

TRANSFORM

MARCIA DASZKO

"A refreshingly honest guide for leaders in today's world. Marcia Daszko will not just shake up some of your long-held beliefs about leadership—she will inspire your thinking and move you to positive action. This book is a life changer for organizations everywhere."
—KEN BLANCHARD, co-author of *The New One Minute Manager*

"*Pivot, Disrupt, Transform* helps readers see that leadership is about—and is brought about—by certain obligations—not that the professional and organizational life, rather a way beyond the silos of conventional wisdom. It did not hesitate to share with me the candidness needed, leading to the same questions, new perspectives, and re-looking at the path that will make the difference between backsliding and progress."
— BARRY Z. POSNER, bestselling author of *The Leadership Challenge*

"Marcia Daszko provides a clear, and well-founded publication, rich with knowledge and tools to cultivate organizations with an open and genuine consideration through dynamically improved collaboration with an energized, gaming, and emphasis. Those who seek about how to share common ground that are needed in applying courage, understanding and purpose, will find Marcia's book relevant and transformative."
— VICE ADMIRAL KEVIN P. GREEN, USN, VP of BRM Allies

"Full of counterintuitive advice, *Pivot, Disrupt, Transform* will shake up your thinking about what really works. Daszko, Daszko will never you more than you played the journey. Get to work to reinvent your path to success."
— DANIEL H. PINK, author of *When*, *Drive*, and *To Sell Is Human*

"*Pivot, Disrupt, Transform* is an important voice to W. Edwards Deming's book *Out of the Crisis*, never a hope to emerge after post-World War II common recovery. With 70 percent of U.S. startups falling each year, and so are too many 500 companies, struggles, mergers and takeovers, Marcia Daszko's book offers leaders a proven antidote. Her provocative questions and diverse therapies explore the outdated thinking and irrelevant systems and processes that are widely unquestioned. It's learned to continue, now unchallenged, to unleashed, just renewing the efforts available to you. Organizations must learn to continually reinvent their foundations and trust and what teamwork success feels as they will continue to fail spectacularly. Or, they can use what Daszko preaches in *Pivot, Disrupt, Transform* today and choose, make, work."
— COLONEL DEBRA M. LEWIS (Ret.), West Point pioneer, positivity and mental toughness expert, combat commander, Harvard MBA

BUSINESS & ECONOMICS
ISBN 978-1-63576-474-1
US $24.99 | CAN $33.99

DIVERSION BOOKS

Chapter 6

Great Leaders STOP Fads and Pivot, Disrupt, and Transform: Abandon These Three Fads

Author: Marcia Daszko

Marcia Daszko is one of the world's leading business strategists and catalysts for leadership and organizational transformation. Her new book, *Pivot Disrupt Transform*, is full of profound, provocative, and contrarian messages that help leaders revolutionize their results. She has 25 years of proven consulting success as CEO of Marcia Daszko & Associates. A protégé of Dr. W. Edwards Deming, she co-founded both the Bay Area Deming User's Group (BADUG) and the In2In Thinking Network. Marcia has been nominated for the international quality Deming Prize award. She is a leadership news columnist for the *Silicon Valley Business Journal*. She works across all sectors, from private to Fortune 500 corporations, non-profits, healthcare, education, and government agencies.

Email: md@mdaszko.com
Website: https://www.mdaszko.com
LinkedIn: https://www.linkedin.com/in/marciadaszko/

Great Leaders STOP Fads and Pivot, Disrupt, and Transform: Abandon These Three Fads

Executives often follow practices simply because "it's the way we've always done it," or because a favorite company did them and their business skyrocketed. Following in the footsteps of others with "best practices" puts you at a disadvantage. Great leaders adopt and implement these three interactive business strategies. They focus on quality, continual improvement, and innovation as their foundation. These are linked with their customers and future markets. They pivot and disrupt old thinking and "best practices" and transform themselves and their organizations.

Start getting better results in your organization by moving away from these management fads:

1. STOP Focusing on the Numbers, Metrics, and the Bottom Line

Instead of focusing on the bottom line, focus on improving or innovating the system that creates the results. If the results need to be different, focus on changing the system. Caring about and understanding the relevance of the bottom line is far different than obsessing over it. When the obsession is the bottom line, the company will not survive.

When executives are focusing on the numbers and reacting to and tampering with them, they are not doing their job. Their job is to create an optimal system and environment for people to do great work and serve customers and new markets. Leaders understand that the systems and processes deliver the results. Blaming, judging, and criticizing people or tampering with the numbers won't improve the results. Change the system.

2. STOP Setting Individual Arbitrary Numerical Goals and Holding Individuals Accountable

Being accountable and being responsible are two different concepts, and each must be applied differently. Leadership is held *accountable* for the system that it created and for the system's results. The people are *responsible* for contributing their part to help the system deliver its outcomes. When individuals are held accountable, the dollars wasted in performance appraisals, performance management, performance improvement plans (PIPs), and recruiting and onboarding new hires is horrendous.

Leaders create a system that can adapt to change and continually improve until it delivers the desired results. They engage the employees in helping make a system that is effective, adds value, makes sense, and serves customers.

3. STOP Using Performance Appraisals, Ratings, and Rankings

Performance appraisals are destructive, particularly those that rank and rate employees. They create internal competition and fear. They do not promote collaboration, teamwork, or the interconnected thinking that provides value. More organizations are self-destructive due to archaic leadership beliefs and policies that promote internal conflict. Great leaders focus on developing and appreciating people, using authentic communication. Performance appraisal systems are full of wrong assumptions and practices that harm people and organizations. As the Hippocratic Oath taken by medical professionals states: "Do no harm."

When leaders STOP well-meaning but toxic practices in their organizations, they can move to transform. Transformation in the context of management of organizations and systems occurs first in individuals and then in the organization.

Transformation is Essential to Achieve a Sustainable Competitive Edge

Transformation has become a popular, overused, and misunderstood word. Executives try to "talk the language" and react. People often confuse transformation with any kind of change, technology breakthrough, innovation, process improvement, or transition. However, few changes are truly transformational. While all transformation is change, not all change is transformation.

Transformation is the creation and change of a whole new form, function, or structure. To transform is to create something that has never existed before and could not be predicted from the past. It is a change in mindset—from limiting beliefs and assumptions to a continually developing, learning, challenging, questioning, and envisioning mindset. The shift is beyond the boundaries of the current thinking. It requires a radical revision, a profound change, a "mind transplant." That takes courage!

Transformation occurs when leaders create a vision for transformation and a system to continually question and challenge beliefs, assumptions, patterns, habits, and paradigms. This needs to be done with the aim of continually developing and applying management theory through the lens of the system of profound knowledge. Transformation happens when people managing a system focus on creating

a new future that has never existed before, and based on continual learning and a new mindset, take different actions than they would have taken in the past.

Leaders have opportunities to experiment, improve, and ultimately, create a system within which their team can be self-motivated enough to contribute willingly. Leaders create possibilities for learning, working, improving, and innovating together.

It takes courage and commitment to challenge old thinking, but great leaders transform themselves and their organizations to innovate and serve current and future markets. How are you thinking and leading? Will you transform?

51

Great leaders provoke new thinking and action for results never before envisioned! They ask questions and challenge the status quo, current beliefs, assumptions, and "best practices."

_____

_____

_____

52

Leaders ask, "What is our compelling purpose? What are we trying to accomplish together?"

_____

_____

_____

53

Great leaders don't try to motivate their employees (which often ends up de-motivating them). They create an environment where people are self-motivated. That's where the real power is!

54

Great leaders pivot and disrupt their own current thinking and practices and transform their organizations so they will be both survivors and innovators.

55

Shake up your long-held beliefs about leadership! They won't work for the future.

56

Leaders pay a price for poor product or service quality! Customers leave. What price can you afford to pay?

57

Leaders want to make a difference in their organization, industry, or society. They find the courage to challenge today's strategies and embrace bold, radical thinking and new actions.

_____

_____

_____

58

Growing an organization means continually investing in and developing your people. People love to learn! Uncover their joy in learning and working together.

59

When you see an organization full of complexity, chaos, stress, waste, and high turnover, those reflect outdated thinking and irrelevant systems and practices. It's time to pivot, disrupt, and transform.

60

Transformation isn't easy, but it is satisfying to sustain the organization, deliver more value to customers, and leave a legacy you can be proud of.

_____

_____

_____

Chapter 7

A People-Centered, Value-Focused Approach to Innovation Management for 21st-Century Organizations

Author: Oliver Yu

Oliver Yu is an internationally recognized expert on technology strategy planning. Prior to 2000, when he founded the STARS Group, a premier innovation consulting firm, he spent 11 years as the director of energy and technology strategies at Stanford Research Institute. His proven methodology for technology portfolio planning has been continuously applied by governments and businesses around the world. Oliver earned a PhD from Stanford University and has authored over 80 technical papers and six books, including *Technology Portfolio Planning and Management*, *Technology Management and Forecasting*, and *Advances in Technology and Innovation Management*. He is a Fellow of the Portland International Center for Management of Engineering and Technology, a co-founder of the International Society of Innovation Methods, and a board member and chair of entrepreneurship and innovation at Technology and Engineering Management Society (TEMS) of IEEE.

Email: oliver.yu@sjsu.edu
Phone: 1 (650) 922-0882
LinkedIn: https://www.linkedin.com/in/oliver-yu-46b97372/

A People-Centered, Value-Focused Approach to Innovation Management for 21st-Century Organizations

Innovations—from the invention of fire and the wheel to agricultural inventions, weaponries, printing press, scientific discoveries, industrial revolution, and ideological evolutions—have been the driving force of civilization. In today's globalized world, continued successful innovation is critical for organizations, from corporations to nations, to survive and thrive. Societies have been greatly transformed by innovations in the last three millennia. Successful innovations must provide value to all people involved in the innovation process. In 21ST-century organizations, we need people-centered, value-focused concepts and tools for innovation management in order to effectively motivate idea creation, incentivize teams to work together effectively, generate returns to investors and other supporters, and provide real and meaningful value to adopters of these innovations.

61

Innovation can be simply defined as an idea implemented with impact, with emphasis on IMPACT.

62

The definition of innovation being an idea implemented with impact applies to innovations in technology, methodology, theory, philosophy, and ideology.

63

Innovation is not a static idea, but a dynamic process involving people, and can be analyzed systematically.

64

The four key participants in the innovation process are the Idea Generator, the Team, Supporters (including regulatory & financial), and Adopters, including the entire supply chain of the product/service developed from the creative idea.

65

Every participant makes decisions on investing time, money, energy, other resources, balancing expected value and risk from participating in the innovation process. Modern portfolio theory can be used to analyze and align these decisions.

66

The heart of innovation management is understanding human needs, which are the basis for the perception of value and risk in the investment decisions made by each participant.

67

The Maslovian model of human needs is not practical. A new model categorizes needs into two dimensions: physical-psychological and security-stimulation. These diversify with increasing physical, financial, intellectual, and spiritual resources.

68

Between 1750 and 2000, real per capita income in industrialized countries increased 100-fold through innovations, which has provided large physical, financial, and intellectual resources to the general population of these countries.

69

In the 21st century, there are three major challenges for organizations: exponential technology change, growing demand for autonomy and meaning by workers, and increasing fragmentation of markets due to diversified needs of adopters.

70

High-impact implementation of creative ideas requires a scenario approach to forecast future changes and the new human needs model to observe, analyze, and understand diversified adopter needs and evolving worker motivations.

Section 3

The Human Side of Silicon Valley

Chapter 8

When the Concern Is Technology, People Make the Difference

Author: Susan G. Schwartz

Susan G. Schwartz, PMP, helps people who are experts in their field unearth their inner leader and develop professional skills, such as relationship building, to better help their organizations grow their business and build strong, effective teams. Recently, she published her first book, *Creating a Greater Whole: A Project Manager's Guide to Becoming a Leader*, which unlocks the not-so-secret secrets of how aspiring managers can become strong leaders. Its practical "outcome-tested" strategies and thought-provoking questions offer organizations and individuals a tool to craft a customized framework to help groups create something larger than themselves. Susan is a recent East Coast transplant to the San Francisco Bay Area and is enjoying her adventures while meeting new people and exploring new places.

Email: sgs@riverbirchgroup.com
Website: www.riverbirchgroup.com
LinkedIn: https://www.linkedin.com/in/susangschwartz/

When the Concern Is Technology, People Make the Difference

One of my favorite career memories is the time that I was in the back seat of a small sedan, hurtling through a blizzard en route from Barneveld, Netherlands to Hamburg, Germany. My Dutch colleagues sitting up front were insistent that I meet the German team of our global software company. They were sure that if they met me in person, they would readily get on board with the project I was spearheading. I needed the support of the German team for my project to succeed. If my Dutch buddies were willing to put life and limb at stake driving in a blizzard, how could I say no? I closed my eyes and held on tight.

Yes, the meeting was successful and the German team became great supporters. One of the reasons I smile when I remember that wild ride is because of how far I'd come from the first years of my career. In the beginning, I'd believed that technology would drive (or drag) business into the future. Somewhere along my professional journey, I realized that technology is simply a tool—it's people who make solutions successful.

Don't misunderstand me: technology offers myriad business solutions that help people increase revenues, minimize costs, and improve productivity. However, it's the ability of humans to participate in collaborative conversations that spurs creative and innovative thinking that:

- identifies the real issues that need to be resolved
- explores and integrates cross-functional solutions
- recognizes and communicates the changes that will occur when the chosen solution is deployed

Combining technical expertise with strong people management skills enable subject matter experts to become extremely valuable assets within their organization. Critical professional, people-focused skills encompass areas such as relationship building, team motivation, conflict resolution, and stakeholder management. These were the skills that I brought with me to that global software company. I hadn't honed these skills early in my career. In fact, a manager once directly told me that I didn't have what it took to be a leader! What he didn't know is that I grew up with three older brothers. If you tell me that I can't do something, I will prove you wrong. Instead of believing him, I took a hard look at how I presented myself, started watching people whose professional style I admired, and began to hone a collaborative leadership style that worked for me and built credibility with others.

When that global software company first brought me on board and asked me to unite 20 different organizations that were operating as independent silos, few people believed that I could succeed. These organizations were spread across 10 countries, five products, and five functional areas. I had been with the company for only four months when my Dutch colleagues drove me to Germany in that blizzard. They were the first people who believed that the vision that I brought was possible. They introduced me to the influential Germans, and by the end of 18 months, our team's effort had positively impacted the schedule, budget, and productivity metrics that were crucial to our business success.

The most significant success started from a simple conversation that identified a potential nine-month software delay and initiated a cross-functional effort that brought the software development schedule back to an on-time delivery. The software development manager had given up hope of fixing the delay. Our collaborative conversation helped him view the challenge from alternate perspectives. It turns out that the issue causing the delay was not a technology challenge, it was a people challenge. We considered a series of "what if" scenarios and identified a shared people resource solution that had never been tried before—and it worked!

Technical experts spend years honing their hard, tangible skills. It is unreasonable to expect them to automatically be expert at intangible professional skills such as building relationships, motivating a diverse team, negotiating for resources, or managing difficult conversations. These professional "human" skills can be developed. The ROI that business leaders will obtain from a focus on professional skills are employees who can better assist with sales and increase team productivity. Increased revenues and decreased costs are only the start as corporate cultures are strengthened, retention rates improve, and companies become known as excellent places to work.

71

Healthy conflict is good. It's how you handle it that makes the difference.

_____
_____
_____

72

One of the deepest secrets leaders rarely share is that we are making it up as we go along.

_____
_____
_____

73

Survival by adaptation evolves solutions and promotes success.

74

Just because it has always been done that way doesn't mean you must continue that way.

75

Failure that provides learning and progress is success. Fail forward!

76

Bad things happen. Strong functional teams come together to create solutions, while dysfunctional teams waste time pointing fingers to assign blame.

77

A poll of top-rated leaders identified continuous learning as a personal goal. One definition for this is "Educated Ignorance," because the more these leaders learned, the more they realized there was much more to learn.

_____

_____

_____

78

Be present and pay attention.

79

Active listening involves probing questions followed by attentive silence to gain understanding.

80

Matrix teams are tough: The team manager has all the responsibility for the project success and no authority for team members who report to other managers.

Chapter 9

Disrupting Workplace Biases

Author: Matthew Cahill

Matthew Cahill is a business consultant with deep expertise in cognitive, social, and workplace biases. He works with businesses to help them make better products, generate more revenue, and foster inclusion. From interpersonal workshops for executives and corporate boards to employee team building, HR process definitions, and inclusive meeting protocols, top-performing companies understand that for a teachable moment to be valuable, it must be both targeted and tailored. Matthew's workshops, speaking engagements, and consulting techniques lead to organizational transformation, empowering individuals to identify their biases, strengthen relationships, and disrupt bias in the workplace.

Email: mjc@percipiocompany.com
Website: https://percipiocompany.com
LinkedIn: https://www.linkedin.com/in/matthewjcahill/

Disrupting Workplace Biases

Bias. It's a word we hear more and more every day in our workplace, in the media, and in our communities. When we hear the word "bias," it automatically seems like a negative thing. If we have bias, that must mean that we are prejudiced.

Let's change that line of thought by distinguishing between conscious and unconscious bias. The Oxford Dictionary defines conscious bias as an intentional act in favor of, or against, one thing, person, idea, or group compared with another, usually in a way that's considered to be unfair or unjustified. This is typically what we think of when we hear the word "bias." Unconscious bias, however, is an unrecognized mental process or categorization that is intimately tied to how the human brain processes information, specifically what neuroscience experts call "cognitive heuristics." The fact is that if we have a brain, we have bias.

Our brain uses bias to protect us, both to literally keep us safe from harm and to protect us from the onslaught of information our brain is dealing with. Our brains navigate 11,000,000 bits of information at any given moment, but our conscious brain can only process 50 bits of information[1] per second. The distance between 50 and 11 million is where unconscious bias resides. We develop mental shortcuts to perform everyday activities, and cognitive biases are the result. Cumulative advances in neuroscience, social psychology, and biology have discovered over 200 named cognitive biases[2]!

Even though cognitive biases are universal, they are not neutral. They can easily lead to social biases in how we interact with each other and can be the seeds of negative institutional biases. Understanding cognitive biases provides us with tools to identify our patterns and our role in perpetuating them. In the workplace, mitigating cognitive biases helps improve decision-making in team environments, promote intellectual curiosity, attract and retain top talent, improve performance, increase innovation, strengthen relationships, and disrupt institutional biases that are negatively impacting both people and performance.

---

[1] https://www.britannica.com/science/information-theory/Physiology
[2] https://en.wikipedia.org/wiki/List_of_cognitive_biases

In my research and through my practice, I've identified five cognitive biases that are the most common in the workplace, each focusing on a different way that we learn, as well as how we make and use categories. These "Frequent 5" form the acronym LEAAP: Like-Me, Egocentric, Availability, Anchoring, and Proximity.

With **Like-Me Bias**, we like people who are like us. We all know this to be true from our everyday interactions with other people. In making small talk with someone we have just met, we look for connections so our brain can rapidly place them into an "in-group" or "out-group." Our brain tries to determine who is a threat and who is an ally, and it makes this decision on limited information. This shortcut can provide a sense of comfort and security. However, it also means that we overvalue people whom we think are like us, and undervalue people whom we think are not like us. The Like-Me Bias can easily lead to establishing informal or formal hiring, collaboration, and promotion practices that further entrench this bias into the employee population and governance structure of an organization.

Egocentric Bias is the belief that "my ideas are obvious and absolute." Egocentric bias can occur when we overvalue our own experience and assume understanding from others. This bias is common in leadership positions or any role where expertise is necessary, like law or medicine. It's easy for any subject matter expert to overvalue their own experience and expertise because this expertise is what their credibility is based upon. It's also often infused with their sense of identity and self-worth. However, to truly vet out the best product ideas, determine the ideal prospects, or allocate company resources, leaders must put aside their egocentric bias and look at multiple points of view. This is vital to avoiding mental mistakes and making better decisions.

Availability Bias occurs when decisions are made based on easy or incomplete ideas without looking at the bigger picture. This bias increases when we are in a rush or are under a high cognitive load. For most of us, this happens every day and all the time as we manage life's complex details and multiple deadlines. When availability bias is in full effect, we take the path of least resistance, and as a result, we make unintentional errors. This might show up as confirmation bias[3], which

---
[3]https://en.wikipedia.org/wiki/Confirmation_bias

is only looking at information that supports what we already know, or the halo effect[4], where we let positive qualities in one area influence our overall perception of someone. Mitigating this strategy means allowing time to consider various points of view and to approach things from different perspectives.

With **Anchoring Bias**, decisions are made from the initial data point, graph, or image to which we are exposed. Once we have this first reference point (whether the reference is factually accurate or not), we calibrate all other information against it. When research participants are "anchored" in a particular direction by including a higher or lower data point, the results of their responses are dramatically different. For example, when asked, "What is the height of the tallest redwood tree?" or "What was Gandhi's age when he died?", responses vary by up to 50%, depending on whether a low or high anchor (in this case, height or age) is included with the initial question. While anchoring bias is an unconscious process in the receiver of communication, it is often used with conscious intent in sales and marketing by those sending the message. A powerful mitigation strategy is to question the source of the initial information (the anchor), as this gets your mind thinking beyond that first data point.

Proximity Bias is when we unconsciously favor whoever is closest in time or space, while undervaluing those in remote locations. This bias can impact people who work remotely or in multiple office locations where one location is perceived as the headquarters. Proximity bias can even occur within a single office. People who have their desks on different floors can suffer a disadvantage due to their relative distance from more influential people. To mitigate proximity bias in meetings, where some participants are physically present and others participate remotely, actively structure the meeting to include the people joining remotely, as well as those in the same physical space. For example, assign a specific role for those who are remote. Don't assume that joining remotely will have the same impact as being there in person because that is rarely the case.

Although we've discussed all these biases in isolation, in real life, they intersect and multiply their combined impact. These unconscious mental processes dictate

---

[4] https://en.wikipedia.org/wiki/Halo_effect

our decisions and even determine with whom we interact and form relationships. The behaviors within these relationships are where we can begin to see and measure the impact of social biases (race, gender, age, culture, etc.). Over time, these social biases can become institutionalized as we consciously or unconsciously decide how we are going to conduct ourselves inside and outside of the workplace. While cognitive biases are universal, they are not neutral. They can easily lead to social biases in how we interact with each other, and can plant the seeds of institutional biases. Although they are related, cognitive, social, and institutional biases are not the same. We must become skilled at recognizing how cognitive biases and cognitive distortions crop up for each of us individually, how they appear in our relationships, and how they are mirrored in the structures around us. Understanding our "hard-wired" cognitive biases will give us the tools we need to identify our patterns and intervene in our role in perpetuating them.

In the workplace, your company's survival depends on understanding bias. Does that seem too bold of a statement? Consider this: Companies that aren't disrupting their biases will naturally fall into patterns of behavior that can lead them to rapid extinction. McKinsey and Company[5] found that companies that have gender diversity were 21% more likely to have increased profitability, and companies with ethnic and cultural diversity were 35% more likely to outperform the norm. Mitigating cognitive biases helps improve decision-making in team environments, promote intellectual curiosity, attract and retain top talent, improve performance, increase innovation, strengthen relationships, and infuse social justice into business practices. There simply is no downside for a business when it comes to raising unconscious biases to a conscious level, where better choices can be made.

---

[5]https://www.mckinsey.com/business-functions/organization/our-insights/delivering-through-diversity

Chapter 9: Disrupting Workplace Biases

81

If you have a brain, you have bias.

82

Culture is best defined as what we do when we're not thinking about it.

83

You're never doing anything (leading, teaching, facilitating, parenting, loving) as good or as bad as you think you are.

_____

_____

_____

84

What we think we know often gets in the way of learning new things.

_____

_____

_____

Chapter 9: Disrupting Workplace Biases

85

As we get older, we must often unlearn and relearn before we can learn and grow.

86

Life is much richer when we live with a willingness to have our hearts broken open (paraphrased from Sister Simone Campbell).

87

Everyone in life teaches you something. Some teach you what to do, others teach you what not to do. You must determine which is which.

_____

_____

_____

Chapter 9: Disrupting Workplace Biases

88

It's impossible to be curious and certain in the same moment.

___

___

___

89

If you live with one foot in yesterday and one in tomorrow, you'll end up pissing all over today.

___

___

___

90

Instead of asking "What's new?" ask "What's best in your life?" The exchange dives beneath the surface and strengthens even a casual relationship.

Chapter 10

For Better Results, Ask Better Questions

Author: Camille Smith

Camille Smith helps leaders and teams generate authentic relationships to achieve results critical for success and sustainability. Her personal mission names her company, Work In Progress Coaching: "Each of us is a 'work in progress'—constantly learning how to contribute, be fully expressed, and produce results worthy of who we are." To deliver client-centered leadership development programs, Camille draws on her experience as an international consultant, a GILD[6] coach, a co-founder of How Women Lead[7], and more than 25 years of serving a diversity of clients[8].

Email: camille@wipcoaching.com
Website: https://wipcoaching.com/
LinkedIn: https://www.linkedin.com/in/camille-smith-a950284/

---

[6] https://www.linkageinc.com/institutes/global-institute-leadership-development.cfm
[7] https://www.howwomenlead.com/
[8] https://wipcoaching.com/the-buzz/

For Better Results, Ask Better Questions

Poor communication is expensive. The average annual loss looks like this: $62 million for companies with 100 thousand employees, $420,000 with 100 employees (www.shrm.org). To solve the problem, begin with the source. The conversations coming out of your mouth that reduce performance are a symptom. Consider the "automatic" ones between your ears that you think don't matter.

When different results are desired, the first thought is: change behavior! While actions are the source of results, focusing solely on changing actions has limited effectiveness. What we've found to be more sustainable is for people to become aware, through a transformative learning process, of the basic structures in which they know, think, and act. By being aware of our automatic thinking and having tools to disrupt it, we can generate breakthroughs in results, not just once but continually.

Perhaps you've heard that if you want to change the results, change the conversation. What does that mean? Do we talk differently? Use different words? Start by asking better questions. Ask: What conversations need to be changed? Ask: Where do actions come from?

Consider this: our actions are determined by how we interpret whatever is happening. For example, if I think (interpret) that a coworker is taking credit for my ideas, I may withhold my ideas when around them for fear that they'll do it again. If I also think that harmony is better than controversy, I will avoid discussing my complaint with the thief. My behavior matches how I see myself, my coworker, and the situation. The problem is that my automatic thinking encourages me to be on guard, fearful, and withdrawn, qualities that do not help me contribute my best.

Okay, you say, *I'll consider that my thinking tells me what I can and can't do.* So, now what? There are two realms of thinking: conscious and unconscious. The unconscious realm is the one that causes much of the self-limiting mischief. It houses unexamined assumptions, conclusions unrelated to current reality, and past-based interpretations. Personal interpretations include: *I have to prove myself. Don't ever question the boss. Be nice. I'm not good enough. Why don't they follow simple instructions? No one listens to me. Don't trust too much.*

You may recognize some of these because they are part of our human design. These automatic, self-limiting conversations won't go away, even when we become aware of them. What we can do is alter our relationship to them so they don't influence our actions.

Just as individuals have automatic, historical thinking, so do organizations. Organizational interpretations sound like this: *We've always done it this way, why change? We're always going to be number one. Sales gets steak; support gets leftovers. Millennials workers need to be reined in.*

What automatic conversations are holding your organization's performance hostage? Leaders and managers are responsible for creating a conversational environment that releases everyone from performance-limiting conversations. In our partnership, you'll learn how to master the conversational environment and create relationships and results that break through automatic thinking to imagine and fulfill compelling new futures.

91

Micromanagement happens when management isn't present. Management is not a police state. It's a state of certainty, clarity, and rigor, founded on the principle of honoring ourselves as our word.

92

The saying, "everything happens for a reason," is only half right. Something happens, then we invent a reason. Make sure that what you invent forwards the future you're committed to, not the past that limits you.

93

We are overwhelmed because we do not know how much we have to do. How to quell overwhelm? List everything. Prioritize against goals, not guilt. Renegotiate. Act and keep your word.

94

If you're afraid to say something because it might break the relationship, that relationship is already broken. Take responsibility. Speak your truth. Listen to theirs. Don't "tap out." Your relationships are the foundation of results.

Chapter 10: For Better Results, Ask Better Questions

95

Automatically being nice hijacks relationships and casts people as fragile. People are not fragile. People are incredible human beings looking for partners to pull off the impossible. Treat them with respect. Say what's true for you.

96

We never wake up saying, "Today, I'm going to make mistakes." Calling something a mistake is an after-the-event interpretation. Effective leaders own the interpretation, clean up any mess and move forward.

97

Work to stamp out anonymity. Why? Because it says: "It's not safe to speak up. I can't own my voice. I must hide my views." Is that enough "why" for you?

_____

_____

_____

98

The background noise in your head has outlived its purpose. There are no tigers outside the cave! Put down your spear, leave the cave, and search for partners to make possibilities happen.

_____

_____

_____

99

Trust is the airbag for your team. Can your team withstand the impact of losing a key player? An unforeseen budget cut? A breach of trust? Build a resilient airbag before you need it. Start now!

_____

_____

_____

100

Both the past and the future only exist in the present when we think about them silently or bring them to life in our conversations. You have the power of language: Choose your time zone wisely!

_____

_____

_____

Chapter 11

The Yin and Yang of a Business Transformation: Culture and Strategic Vision

Author: Amit Patel

Amit Patel is an innovative strategist, certified organizational change practitioner, and an organizational transformation executive with over 20 years of global experience. As the founder and managing director of the Mythos Group, he has led a variety of global business transformations for Fortune 100, Fortune 500, and startup companies. Amit serves as a trusted advisor to C-level and senior executives committed to making strategic change actionable, impactful, and lasting. He partners with clients to improve their organizational capabilities and boost organizational effectiveness while empowering human capital to decrease costs and catapult profitability. Amit firmly believes that strategy, organizational change, and global business transformations go hand-in-hand, and that only by working together can the organization be propelled to the next level. His clients praise him for his value and purpose, subject matter expertise, approachability, confidence in dealing with tough ambiguous situations, patience, and innovative thought leadership.

Email: amit.patel@mythosgroupinc.com
Website: https://mythosgroupinc.com/
LinkedIn: https://www.linkedin.com/in/amitpatelstrategyocm/

The Yin and Yang of a Business Transformation: Culture and Strategic Vision

Globally, organizations are faced with a business environment characterized by greater marketplace volatility, frequent economic disruptions, and organizational change. In light of evolving customer behaviors, emerging disruptive technologies, and shifting regulatory policies, there is a clear imperative to transform or risk becoming extinct. It is almost inconceivable that billion-dollar enterprises such as Toys 'R' Us, Borders Books, Blockbuster Video, Circuit City, and Radio Shack no longer exist. Experts attribute the extinction of these companies to their failure to transform in the midst of market changes. According to studies referenced by a *Harvard Business Review* article [1]:

- 75% of the S&P's top 500 companies will drop off of the list in the next 15 years.
- One in three companies will delist in the next five years.
- The "topple rate" of industry leaders falling from their perch has doubled in a generation.

To stay relevant in today's economy and to prevent extinction, organizations need to continually evolve through well-thought-out business transformations, with an emphasis on capacity building and change management. Every organization must assess their ability to withstand the marketplace entry of disruptive companies such as Airbnb, Dropbox, Fitbit, Hulu, Lyft, Pinterest, Snapchat, Spotify, Twitter, and Uber—billion-dollar empires that didn't even exist ten years ago. These new entrants to their markets shifted paradigms to fill niches ignored by existing companies, those that could have done the same had they been attuned to these possibilities.

What is Business Transformation?

Google "business transformation," and you'll discover a plethora of definitions. So, what does business transformation really entail? In an organizational context, it is a profound and radical change that orients an organization in a new direction and takes it to an entirely different level of effectiveness. *Harvard Business Review* suggests that there are at least three different types of transformations [2]:

- Operational—doing what you do better, faster, or cheaper by leveraging new technologies and approaches to improve efficiency. For example, companies that are "going digital" fit into this category.
- Operational Model/Core Transformation—doing what you do in a fundamentally different way. Netflix is a great example of this. Over the last five years, Netflix has shifted from sending DVDs through the mail to streaming video content through the web. It has also expanded from simply distributing other people's content to investing heavily in its own content creation.
- Strategic—changing the very essence of your company. For example, Google expanded from search engine to driverless car, and Apple extended from computers to consumer gadgets.

For our purposes, "business transformation" means proactively and strategically ensuring that a business has the sustainable capacity to continually meet its mission and goals despite inevitable internal and external challenges. It involves making fundamental changes in how business[9] is conducted in order to:

- increase revenue and market share
- reduce operating costs
- improve customer satisfaction
- cope with shifts in the business environment

Business transformation is often achieved by one or more of the following:

- redesigning business processes and realigning the way people do their work
- increased focus on innovation
- implementing transformative technologies
- focusing on stakeholder engagement and customer satisfaction
- strengthening the organization's culture

Typically, business transformation is a journey that can take months or years. Irrespective of whether an organization's transformation requires operational,

---
[9]https://en.wikipedia.org/wiki/Commerce

model/core, or strategic transformation, begin with a gap analysis. Define where the business wants to be, clearly assess where it is today, and then bridge the gap between the two.

The Yin: Lead with Culture in Mind

Organizational culture is driven by people's belief systems and is often tied to underlying emotional constructs. Culture cannot be changed by simply telling people to change their beliefs, but rather by helping people understand the necessity of change and then guiding them to construct and internalize an alternative belief system and a new set of behaviors consistent with the desired change. This must occur on both the individual and collective levels.

To reap the benefits of a business transformation, leaders must take a "culture first" approach. Attempting to implement new behaviors and performance measurements without addressing the underlying culture is simply counterproductive. In times of uncertainty, even well-intentioned employees may slip back into old, undesirable behaviors.

Business transformation is a significant undertaking that requires all employees of an organization to work harmoniously together—and it all begins with the organization's culture.

The Yang: Getting the Right Strategy and Buy-in is Critical

Getting employees on board with a successful business transformation starts with an executive's ability to set and communicate a strategic vision. In the *Oracle/Forbes* Insights survey, 51% of executives surveyed cited support from leadership as a key factor in the success of business transformation projects. This strategic vision serves as a project's "North Star."[3] If you don't know where your business transformation is going, you will never get there.

A business transformation's strategic vision provides a clear and feasible picture of what the future looks like. It provides essential motivation for the organization's stakeholders to let go of the past, work hard in the present, and embrace the future. Business transformations fail when this strategic vision has not been widely shared with the organizational stakeholders and lacks their buy-in, and real buy-in involves an element of co-creation. Involvement encourages stakeholders to embrace change, in spite of the work that it entails, because they have personal ownership of both the transformation and the future that is being co-created.

A successful business transformation is done "with and by," not "to," an organization's stakeholders.

Yin and Yang Alignment Drives Success!
A strong culture (the Yin) that aligns with a specific vision (the Yang) is a winning combination. In your organization's transformative journey, what are you doing to not only strengthen the Yin and the Yang, but to also align them?

[1] What Do You Really Mean By Business "Transformation?" HBR, Scott D. Anthony, February 29, 2016
[2] ibid
[3] Why Business Transformation Fails and How to Ensure It Doesn't, Forbes, Amy Westervelt, et. al., January 23, 2015

101

"Strategy" is a set of choices that enables an organization to create a holistic winning environment and become the best version of itself.

102

Organizational culture starts with what people do, why they do it, and how they do it.

103

There is a strong correlation between an organization's strategy and its culture.

104

In the digital world, organizational culture matters more than ever. As a whole, an organization must unlearn many behaviors that led to their success, and learn new, more effective ones.

105

Leadership and employee potential can be maximized by leveraging emotional intelligence (EQ).

106

Nimble organizations become brilliant. When there is a clear vision, willingness to embrace radical change, teamwork, and collaboration, wonderful things can happen.

107

Employees are the biggest competitive advantage of any organization. Many organizations espouse this view, but only the wise few put it into practice.

_____

_____

_____

108

Success isn't achieved without experiencing a fair share of failures. Learn from them and keep going!

109

Certifications are valuable, but nothing trumps intelligent use of real-life work experience.

110

They may be rare, but successful transformations do exist! Your organization can be successfully transformed if you have a clear strategic vision and four key elements aligned to it: culture, leadership, organization, and employees.

Chapter 12

The Right Questions to Ask Yourself When Launching a New Startup Business

Author: Tom Okada

Tom Okada is an experienced executive in building and managing global teams and business in the technology industry. His career includes leadership roles in engineering and business development in various technology areas such as automotive, mobile devices, IoT, robotics, semiconductors, and embedded software, with a strong global business network. Tom served as a board member of Motorola Japan, Aplix IP Holdings Corporation, and Ecrio Inc.; CEO of Zeemote Inc.; various VP roles in Azingo and Tortuga Pacific; and most recently, executive director of Boston-based WiTricity Corporation. He is a founding member of Silicon Valley Alliances, which helps companies globalize and innovate. He also serves as a mentor for startup companies through Japan's NEDO TCP and NEP programs, Kyoto University's iCAP program, and the Next Innovator program sponsored by Japan's METI. Tom has a BS in electrical engineering from Arizona State University and holds four US patents. Born and raised in Kyoto, Japan, and educated in the US, he lives in the San Francisco Bay area.

Email: tom@siliconvalleyalliances.com
Website: https://SiliconValleyAlliances.com
LinkedIn: https://www.linkedin.com/in/tom-okada-16044a/

The Right Questions to Ask Yourself When Launching a New Startup Business

People start a new business for various reasons and motivations. When driven by a selfish personal agenda, it can get initial traction, but later, it often fails to attract employees and customers and sometimes ends up failing completely. I have seen not only startups but also big companies fall into the trap of greed and fear-driven management, which stifles innovation, creates lack of focus on customers, and invites getting disrupted out of the market. It's important to start with why—your motivation—and focus on the value your new business is creating for society and customers *before* jumping into the product or solution (the what) and implementation (the how). Even when considering technology and product-driven businesses, it's never too late to get back to the basics and ask the right questions.

111

Know yourself: What makes you happy?

___

112

Imagine what you want to be, where you want to be, in 5 to 10 years. Is your goal making you and other people happy, or is it just to satisfy your ego?

Chapter 12: The Right Questions to Ask Yourself When Launching a New Startup Business

113

For your new business: What problem are you trying to solve and why?

_____
_____
_____

114

Who are your target customers? Can you see their faces?

_____
_____
_____

115

What is the addressable TAM? Market size? Potential share of your business in that market?

_____

_____

_____

116

What are the other available solutions or competitors, and why is your solution competitive?

_____

_____

_____

Chapter 12: The Right Questions to Ask Yourself When Launching a New Startup Business

117

Can you attract the best people? Can you work with people who have better knowledge and skill than yourself?

_____
_____
_____

118

Can you allow others to also lead and expand your business?

_____
_____
_____

119

What is your POC (Proof of Concept) or MVP (Minimum Viable Product) to prove that your solution is suited to solving the problem or filling customer needs?

_____

_____

_____

120

What do you need to get to PoC or MVP? Required people, funding, schedule?

_____

_____

_____

Chapter 13

Sail to Career Success through Servant Leadership

Author: Patricia Corcoran

Patricia is an IT management consultant specializing in employee engagement, program management, and project leadership. For the past 20 years, Patricia's experience has spanned all aspects of program, project, and contract management in both private and public sectors, with project sizes in the $500,000 to $500 million range. Clients include financial institutions, biotech, healthcare, regulatory agencies, research, insurance advisory agencies, federal and state governments, and medical schools. She has earned certifications in SAFe Advanced Scrum Master, ITIL v3, Six Sigma, PMP®, and contract management.

Patricia has an impressive success rate leading onshore and offshore software development teams using both agile and waterfall methodologies. This includes management of financials, contract compliance, resources, purchasing, third-party vendors, qualification regulatory compliance, product development and delivery strategy, risk, and change management. Her collaborative approach, following the principles of servant leadership, results in continuing relationships with many clients after project delivery. Patricia is also a sailor, scuba diver, and snow skier. She has gone diving in Belize, Tahiti, the Philippines, Mexico, the Cayman Islands, the British Virgin Islands, Bimini, Bonaire, and Hawaii.

Email: pcorcoran27@yahoo.com
LinkedIn: https://www.linkedin.com/in/patriciacorcoranpmp/

Sail to Career Success through Servant Leadership

Teamwork is the key to attaining a challenging goal. When racing sailboats, the crew must act as a machine, each individual performing their own part, alert and responsive to the changing conditions and the tactician's advice. Success is dependent on these critical components: completion of all of the prep work for the sailing vessel and its rigging and the crew's readiness; clear communications; cooperative teamwork; the ability to quickly pivot to stay on course; and commitment to the success of the "team," not an individual. All these elements are crucial. When an organization (the ship) has a culture with teamwork at the top with a vision and shared goals (the skipper) and crucial interactions and communication (the tactician), these conspire to create a strong foundation for successful planning and execution (the crew).

121

The value of a person resides in what they give, not in what they are capable of receiving.

_____

_____

_____

122

Encourage one another. Many times, a word of praise, thanks, appreciation, or cheer has kept people on their feet.

_____

_____

_____

123

Managers light a fire under people. Leaders light a fire in people.

124

Nothing else can quite substitute for a few well-chosen, well-timed, sincere words of praise. They're free — and worth a fortune!

125

We shall never know all the good that a simple smile can do.

126

Don't judge each day by the harvest you reap, but by the seeds you plant.

127

Ethical leaders are people-oriented and aware of how their decisions impact others. They use their power and authority to serve the greater good instead of self-serving interests — a win/win for employees and the organization.

128

The hallmark of a servant leader is encouragement. A true servant leader says, "Let's go do it!", not, "You go do it."

129

The five most important words: "You did a great job."

130

If you make a mistake, admit it. Then keep going, learning from each mistake and failing forward.

Section 4

Silicon Valley All Over Planet Earth

Chapter 14

The Global Epidemic of Disengaged Employees & Dysfunctional Organizations

Author: Kimberly Wiefling

Kimberly Wiefling helps people achieve what seems impossible but is merely difficult. She's the founder of Wiefling Consulting and co-founder of Silicon Valley Alliances. She wrote a project management book that has been popular globally for over a decade, *Scrappy Project Management: The 12 Predictable and Avoidable Pitfalls Every Project Faces*[10], which was also published in Japanese by Nikkei Business Press[11]. Kimberly is the executive editor of a series of Scrappy Guides[12], most recently, *Scrappy Women in Business* and *Scrappy Campaigning*. Her expertise includes global leadership and team effectiveness, program and project management, creativity and innovation, and organizational culture. Kimberly is wildly enthusiastic about working with people and teams who are committed to solving global problems, profitably and thus sustainably, in order to make a powerful positive difference on Planet Earth.

Email: kimberly@siliconvalleyalliances.com
Websites: SiliconValleyAlliances.com, KimberlyWiefling.com, Wiefling.com
LinkedIn: https://www.linkedin.com/in/scrappykimberlywiefling/

---

[10] http://www.amazon.com/o/ASIN/1600050514/
[11] http://www.amazon.co.jp/o/ASIN/4822283941/
[12] http://wiefling.com/scrappy-books/

The Global Epidemic of Disengaged Employees & Dysfunctional Organizations

Early in my career I was a new product development program manager at HP's Scientific Instruments Division in the heart of Silicon Valley. The first project I led was a critical product redesign with a demanding schedule, so I was dismayed to see this sign hanging at the desk of one of my team members: "15 Years 'til Retirement—Pace Yourself." Rather than being passionately committed to our work together, this person was looking forward to escaping his job so he could finally start enjoying his life. Gallup would describe him as "not engaged," but to me he was yet another risk to our imperiled project.

What is employee engagement? Engaged employees are not merely wage slaves—they feel a positive emotional connection to their organization, and will contribute discretionary effort to their work. Globally nearly 90% of workers are either NOT engaged or are actively *disengaged*—meaning they are actively working against their own organizations! In the US, where engagement is highest, it still averages a pathetic 30%! Even in the world-famous Silicon Valley, the birthplace of chip innovations (circuits, not potatoes) for which it was named, employee engagement is often "less than suboptimal," with people looking forward to their company's IPO so they can quit the jobs they've been enduring as they "rest and vest." You can think of employees who are not engaged as a huge hidden tax on each and every business.

SMART PEOPLE AND GREAT TECHNOLOGY ARE NOT ENOUGH! I live just a short drive from companies like Tesla, eBay, Apple, Google, Cisco Systems, Adobe, and PayPal. Living and working in Silicon Valley has provided me with tremendous opportunities to witness up close how businesses start, then grow and flourish, or falter and fail. Interestingly, the old Sun Microsystems sign is still visible on the back of the famous Facebook sign, a living reminder of what can happen to companies that were once wildly successful.

Please don't assume that failures are the result only of challenges like technology, products, markets, or strategy. I'm a physicist by education, and I made that mistake early in my career. To do so is to miss an incredibly important piece of the puzzle. Many threats that businesses face are completely and utterly human.

Organizations here are composed of brilliant, talented, diverse, and well-educated people. Nevertheless, they often struggle to achieve results due to what some of my techie friends call "the touchy-feely crap." Having also worked abroad with people from about 50 different countries in a wide range of industries, including pharmaceuticals, concrete, plastics, and whiskey, I can tell you that the human challenges we face in Silicon Valley are shared globally. While products, technology, and market fit are certainly vital aspects of successful businesses, widespread workplace dysfunctionality strikes me as the greatest missed opportunity because it's entirely predictable and largely preventable.

According to one study published in MIT Sloan's management journal[13] [1], over 80% of global teams self-reported as failing to reach their own goals, and the most common causes of failure in these teams were:

- lack of trusting relationships
- failure to overcome communication barriers (and this is not limited to language and culture)
- unclear goals
- misalignment between individual and team priorities

Look at this list once more. Whose responsibility is it to ensure that teams build strong, trusting relationships and work together effectively toward clear, shared goals upon which all team members are aligned? This is entirely a failure of leadership! (Notice that I didn't say management. There's a big difference between leadership and management. Both are important, but I've never met anyone who liked being *managed*!)

TOXIC TALENT AND LACKLUSTER LEADERSHIP. Sure, there are other contributing factors, but let's not be so quick to forgive this tragic absence of effective leadership in the global work environment. Even a brief peek into the inner workings of many organizations reveals that they are not teams, but merely groups of people working together. Their managers are not leaders, and their organizations are dysfunctional by design, thanks to power poisoning and hierarchies that breed what have come to be known as "bossholes." (Yup, there's a whole new word for people who suck their employees' will to live!) Their cynicism-inducing values may be posted on the wall, but unless

---

[13] https://sloanreview.mit.edu/article/building-an-effective-global-business-team/

they're willing to fire their best engineer for violating those principles, their values are worthless, even a liability to a healthy organizational culture. The painful consequences of this dysfunction often include high turnover, low productivity, missed opportunities, delayed product launches, and less-than-delighted customers.

With only a fraction of workers truly committed to their work, many organizations achieve success through a combination of heroics, diving catches, miracles, and luck. Some of these accidental achievers ask me, "Kimberly, if our company is so screwed up, why are we successful?" Why, indeed! Lucky for them most of their peers are equally mediocre.

Surely the people responsible for such wasteful misery would recognize their toxic—and sometimes "talk-sick"—impact on their colleagues and change their behavior, right? Unfortunately, often no one feels responsible for this needless suffering. When I work with individual employees, they say, "Sure, Kimberly, we want to make the changes you're suggesting, but it's our managers who are really the cause of these problems." When I challenge managers on these workplace issues, they often point to their executives as the real cause of their difficulties. Executives then point to the CEO, who—heartbroken to think that they might be to blame for this tragic loss of opportunity—confides that the board, investors, shareholders, or other influences are at the root of these problems. Or sometimes they blame their people, to which I respond, "Okay, suppose I discover that *you* are somehow contributing to the dysfunction. How do you want me to tell you?" Their response determines whether I agree to work with them or light my hair on fire and run out the door screaming.

MANAGE COWS, LEAD PEOPLE! What's preventing business leaders all over Our World from adopting what is clearly common sense, not to mention in the long-term best interests of customers, shareholders, and employees? It's been proven beyond a shadow of a doubt that companies with higher employee engagement scores also enjoy better customer satisfaction scores, higher quality, lower employee absenteeism and turnover, and increased profitability. Only a cynic—or someone who's never worked in a dysfunctional organization (which is pretty much someone who's never worked)—will be asking if this is causation or correlation. The research is clear that the biggest contributor to a lack of engagement is a person's direct manager. [2] So, why aren't effective managers, admired leaders, engaged employees, and healthy organizational cultures as common as blades of grass? They could be! It's been known for decades how to do better. There's nothing standing between us and highly engaged, motivated, and productive teams, except perhaps the discipline to spend time on what matters most.

Let's all get busy doing the real work of management: leading! Could we do something more strategic first thing in the morning other than checking email? Might we find better ways to spend our time besides meaningless meetings where the only thing we decide is to meet again? If so, we'd have an excellent opportunity to dramatically improve business results and even—dare I say—enjoy our work. Start with a purpose beyond profit and a mission that matters. Implement commonsense people leadership and business management approaches proven to deliver results predictably and repeatedly. Recognize and sincerely appreciate people's contributions to the organization. This practical approach has the power to truly engage employees, inviting and inspiring people to be strongly committed to shared goals that would be impossible for any individual to achieve, but are inevitable for a true team.

S.T.O.P! But don't just rush off and start doing things willy-nilly! Replace the all-too-common, adrenaline-soaked rush to solution with enough planning to optimize your results.

- Stop
- Think
- Organize
- Plan

At the very least, this means spending a few minutes considering:

- Big WHY—What's your purpose?
- Big WHO—Who are the stakeholders involved or impacted? (This often involves a complex universe of conflicting interests that seem truly impossible to satisfy.)
- Big WHAT—What exactly would "success" look like through the eyes of your key stakeholders?
- MEASURES—What would be the measures of success through the eyes of your stakeholders?

- Then, and only then, create your Big HOW!—This should be a draft plan filled with plenty of experiments, prototypes, and other opportunities to learn, adjust, and pivot.
- EXECUTE with excellence—Take necessary risks, learn from mistakes, and fail forward.

Unfortunately, given a choice about how much time to spend planning before diving into any challenge, most humans will choose . . . wait for it . . . *zero*! Yup, no time spent planning. Just start doing things! After all, no code is written while planning, no products ship, and no revenue is booked. But an optimal amount of planning more than doubles your chances of success in complex tasks, and can improve results for even a seemingly simple one. (Ever go to the grocery store without a list and discover you've forgotten a vital item upon returning home?)

CROSSING THE KNOWING-DOING GAP. Look, I don't expect reading this to change you. If knowing how to do something were enough, we'd all be rich and thin. There's always a reason well-intentioned, educated, experienced professionals are doing the opposite of what they know makes sense. Frequently, it's because they are really busy and can't possibly do what needs to be done until someone *else* changes first—usually their boss or someone in a different department. In fact, a well-researched book called *The Knowing-Doing Gap* was written by two Stanford University professors who noticed that their colleagues at the Stanford Graduate School of Business didn't follow *their own teachings* when they themselves led companies. What is the source of this gap between knowing and doing? Here are a few:

- Learned helplessness: This is "It's not my fault!" and "They are doing it to me" thinking.
- Fear of failure: If you're not allowed to fail, you must be very careful what you start.
- Aversion to planning: As I've mentioned, given a choice, people prefer not to plan . . . at *all*!
- Instinct for competition: A win-lose frame is the first assumption that many people make in any situation involving another person, even when win-win can yield more benefits.

Knowing *how*, by itself, changes *nothing*! Over 70% of business failures have been attributed to an inability to execute.

TAKE PERSONAL RESPONSIBILITY FOR BUILDING AN ENGAGING WORKPLACE. Peter Drucker reportedly said, "Culture eats strategy for breakfast." An organization's culture is as invisible as the air we breathe and as inescapable as gravity. But sick, twisted, dysfunctional organizations didn't spring unbidden from the earth, and they weren't deposited by alien lifeforms. *We* create these workplace cultures. The upside of this scary proposition is that we also have the power to change them for the better.

If we acknowledge the dark side of organizations and our own contributions to them, we can create a future where individuals, teams, and organizations generate great results by design rather than by chance. Investors might be happy with a 10% success rate for the companies they invest in, but do you really want to accept those odds? You needn't. We can do better. Act like a leader. The difference between someone occupying a management position and being a truly effective leader is that real leaders have the discipline to do what's required, whether they feel like it or not—no excuses! How we feel is a poor guide to what we must do to succeed.

You may be asking yourself, "Could it really be this simple?" Simple, yes. Easy, no. Using this approach, you can make what seems impossible merely difficult, then possible, and enable your team to achieve together what no one could do alone. (Email me if you'd like a one-page overview of this commonsense methodology.)

WHAT'S AT STAKE? PLANETARY TRANSFORMATION! Businesses were not created to exploit workers and generate fortunes for their owners. They exist to solve problems—and to do it profitably so they can continue to solve these problems year after year. In the same way, global businesses solve global problems, and bring people together across borders and boundaries of every kind to work together in ways that elude governments. With so much at stake, this is no time to pace yourself! With so much to gain, not only for your people but also for our world, we need to *KEEP GOING*! And when we do fail, let's fail for new and more exciting reasons!

[1] Vijay Govindarajan and Anil K. Gupta, "Building an Effective Global Business Team," *MIT Sloan Management Review*, Summer 2001
[2] Jim Clifton and Jim Harter, "It's the Manager: Gallup finds the quality of managers and team leaders is the single biggest factor in your organization's long-term success," May 2019

131

The foundation of a wildly successful business is a purpose beyond profit on a mission that matters. There's no downside to moving beyond purely mercenary motives. Purpose-driven businesses make more money!

132

Leadership isn't the same as management, and a "group of people" isn't the same as a real team. Confuse these at your peril! Nobody wants to be managed. Manage schedules and budgets, not people or teams. Lead people, manage cows!

133

Effective leaders are willingly followed by others. We've known for decades that effective leadership is authentic, honest, forward-looking, inspiring, and competent. Leaders aren't born — they choose leadership.

134

No matter your position in the org chart or title on your business card, you can lead from any chair simply by practicing the 30 proven leadership behaviors in "The Leadership Challenge" by Posner & Kouzes.

135

Leadership is about behaviors, not beliefs. The best leaders on Planet Earth A.C.T. — Act like a leader, Communicate like a leader, and Think like a leader. It's simple but not easy.

136

Money is like oxygen: If you have enough, you don't appreciate it, and if you don't, that's all you think about. Recognize, appreciate, and celebrate people's contributions (including learning from mistakes) with more than money!

137

Humans tend to rush to solutions and actions without doing any planning whatsoever. You can dramatically increase your odds of success and the quality of your results if you S.T.O.P. — Stop, Think, Organize and Plan — then GO!

_____

_____

_____

138

Whenever results matter, consider the Big WHY (purpose) —> the Big WHO (stakeholders) —> the Big WHAT (goals) and the Measures of "Success" through the eyes of the stakeholders BEFORE considering the Big HOW and execution.

139

Facts, logic, and knowing how are not enough. If they were, nobody would smoke! Leaders care. Find something you care about more than your comfort, and then choose to be a leader.

140

The #1 factor that separates successful individuals, teams, and organizations from mediocre ones is the DISCIPLINE to DO what's proven to work and what's required every day, day after day, whether you feel like it or not. KEEP GOING!

Chapter 15

Working with Agility:
How Executive Leaders Can Spread Silicon Valley Magic

Author: Annie Sheehan

Annie Sheehan is an experienced executive coach, with 25 years of project delivery experience in Europe, Asia Pacific, and the USA. During the last 10 years, she has focused on coaching executives to turn their ideas and problems into choices, their choices into manageable plans, and those plans into reality.

Using an agile mindset with established project delivery practices, Annie helps organizations find ways to deliver value in manageable chunks using simple, repeatable processes. Her personal mantra is to "maximize life and stay sane."

Annie has been collaborating with Kimberly Wiefling since 2014 and had the privilege of experiencing a Silicon Valley immersion in 2015. She has since taken those Silicon Valley insights and applied them with her clients and colleagues in Australia and around the world.

Email: annie@annie-sheehan.com
Website: https://www.annie-sheehan.com
LinkedIn: https://www.linkedin.com/in/annie-c-sheehan

Working with Agility: How Executive Leaders Can Spread Silicon Valley Magic

Business leaders worldwide are agitated. While they wait an eternity for their latest projects to deliver, executives watch their profits eroded by technology competitors who are devouring their supply chain. Many leaders want to reproduce the success of these entrepreneurs that seem to have been "born agile." At the heart of agile is a promise to deliver value to customers early, in incremental chunks. Value is created using proven healthy routines and rituals (like two-week delivery sprints, daily short stand-up meetings, and retrospectives to capture lessons learned) with an attitude of adapting your approach when things don't go quite as planned.

Since the publication of the Agile Manifesto in 2001, software development has improved in terms of speed, cost, quality, and customer value. These delivery improvements have coincided with a surge in the popularity of the behavioral psychology movement. Business management schools have blended these to promote the concept of "organizational agility." While we are trying to keep up with a fast pace of change, we are expected to be striving and thriving, resilient, hopeful, and determined. These expectations can seem both unrealistic and exhausting to leaders and their teams.

So, if you want to reap the benefits of organizational agility (aka "the agile promise") without a PhD in computing or pushing yourself to breaking point, where do you start? Fortunately, many Silicon Valley companies of all sizes exhibit characteristic patterns of behavior that you can leverage for your rapid success.

Common Silicon Valley Success Factors

1. Learn by Doing

They set up the right environment and disciplines and then live them. It isn't just inspirational posters on the wall with no action. You can start with a visual management dashboard and a daily stand-up meeting. If you don't know anything about agile ways of working, get some foundational knowledge. Shadow a capable team or attend training geared toward businesspeople solving customer problems vs. technology-centric training. This experience will help you understand what "good" looks and feels like so you know when you are achieving it in your environment.

2. Collaboration for innovation

- Solopreneurs team up with trusted friends to bring a fresh perspective to their service offering.
- Small organizations use collaborative working spaces (like Plug and Play Tech Center, the birthplace of Dropbox and PayPal) to gain energy by working alongside other motivated individuals and businesses.
- Larger organizations like Facebook, have customized collaborative spaces. Facebook headquarters' rooftop garden includes play spaces with games and facilitation spaces with creative seating.

Regardless of the size of your collaborative ventures, ensure that they are tied back to real-life problem-solving, the underpinning culture encourages trust and constructive conflict among team members. Call out "fake agile" (where there are inspirational posters with incongruent behavior), and be prepared to change the organization's culture if you need to.

3. Take Time to Reflect on Lessons Learned

Attend retrospectives and create a knowledge store of those insights to understand patterns and trends to pre-empt problems. Ask curious questions and listen to understand rather than listening to respond. Hang out with people who disagree with you, and engage in healthy conflict to challenge your thinking.

Finally, allow yourself the luxury of focus that agile prioritization affords you. Drop those less important pieces and embrace the JOMO (Joy of Missing Out). You will get more done and be happier for it!

Good luck!

Suggested further reading:

- *Mindset*[14] by Carol Dweck (Learn by Doing)
- *The Five Dysfunctions of a Team*[15] by Patrick Lencioni (Healthy conflict in teams)

[14]https://www.amazon.com/Mindset-Psychology-Carol-S-Dweck/dp/0345472322/
[15]https://www.amazon.com/Five-Dysfunctions-Team-Leadership-Fable/dp/0787960756/

141

New labels for proven principles: In Silicon Valley, the word "Agile" doesn't need to be spoken. "Agile" routines and rituals are accepted as a normal way of working.

142

It's easier to create change when you are part of a movement. In Silicon Valley, there's a critical mass of people collaborating and delivering. Without followers, you're a lone nut. Maximize your exposure to these entrepreneurial people.

143

When people feel psychologically safe, they are more productive. In Silicon Valley, people are not afraid to experiment. It is a way of life. An experiment fails, not a person. What can you do to create safety for your teams?

144

Innovation is not a forced formula. In Silicon Valley, although creative workspaces are important, innovation happens everywhere. Rumor has it that brainstorming over lunch at Buck's of Woodside resulted in the creation of the Tesla car!

145

Be an approachable and grounded human, even when you're a famous CEO. We are all just flesh and blood and bone. Tim Draper, founder of Draper University, is a great role model.

146

Success is not final and failure is not fatal. You can fall out of popularity and you can also make a comeback. Steve Jobs and his rise, fall, and resurrection with Apple is a great example of this.

147

Employing a sense of playfulness brings joy, energy, and innovation. Silicon Valley companies encourage you to connect with your inner child, like Google and their garden full of life-size Androids.

148

Embrace diversity in all its forms: age, gender, ethnicity, skills, style, etc. Silicon Valley's definition of "normal" is expansive and inclusive. Master the obvious and explore the unusual to give you that competitive edge.

_____

_____

149

Actively listen to your helpful critics. The best Silicon Valley companies ignore their internet trolls and harsh critics (haters gonna hate). Invite helpful critics into your inner circle to refine your service offering and stay relevant.

_____

_____

150

Keep the faith. Remind yourself of the Silicon Valley magic to keep your entrepreneurial spirit alive when negativity threatens to overcome your work. Keep a few inspiring stories, useful statistics, and meaningful photos nearby.

Chapter 16

Leading from Any Chair and Virtually Anywhere!

Author: Jeff Richardson

Jeff Richardson is a "transformational engineer" with over 20 years of experience helping tech leaders innovate and scale their business through strategic planning, design thinking, and company/group culture.

Primary focus is always on getting the leadership team aligned and committed to a share vision and strategy. Then we set off to sync up the rest of the organization and partners to reestablish common goals and prioritize projects that will expedite the timeline. Jeff's teamwork and experiential learning skill sets are helpful in engaging diverse groups, both in face-to-face events or using online platforms. Use this next change project to also set new expectations for utilizing web meeting agendas that are interactive, decision oriented, and viewed as "a valuable use of our time."

Jeff's expertise includes design thinking for TCS's clients and as a product launch consultant in the defense industry and the M&A common process implementation. Clients include Kaiser IT, General Electric, SETI Institute, Yamaha, Takeda, and Toray. He's also designed programs for Stanford, UCSC-Ext, and Keio and Kyoto Universities.

Email: Jeff@EmpoweredAlliances.com
Website: https://EmpoweredAlliances.com
LinkedIn: https://www.linkedin.com/in/richardsonjeff/

Leading from Any Chair and Virtually Anywhere!

Technology innovations lead to only marginal improvements in team effectiveness despite their immense potential to engage knowledge workers locally and around the world. What's undermining this evolution is a leadership challenge that has everyone scrambling just to keep up and no bandwidth to build a foundation from which to innovate. Teamwork that transcends organizational and geographical boundaries will require a different leadership mindset to think more creatively and satisfy a wider set of stakeholder desires. Insightful solutions can only thrive in an environment where trust and emotional safety are high. Someone must step up to the challenge, and it's not always the formal leader of the team. Today's complex work dynamics require a small group of informal leaders to take on more responsibility for shaping an operating culture that is both adaptable and rhythmic. Leaders must work together to establish principles and team habits that enable fast, focused decision making as a starting point, in addition to constant, clear, and concise communication as the fabric that will hold it all together under pressure. Here are key insights from my experiences helping shape work cultures to be more effective, fun, and sustainable.

151

New partnership models will blur organizational boundaries, increasing the need for leaders with the agility to adapt to ambiguity. Learn to stretch yourself in service of these new teams, and establish yourself as an invaluable resource.

152

Play an active role in bridging the gaps among the people who must make partnerships work at an operational level and you'll make fast friends and establish your name in the minds of executives for both companies!

153

Seek out formal and informal leadership responsibilities to help set the tone for communication from the beginning and establish healthy team habits that focus on more effective ways to work together.

154

Develop strong relationships with new colleagues from partnering groups by making time to connect on a personal level, communicating consistently throughout the project, and delivering on commitments that you make publicly.

155

Insist on sharing feedback early on, and be consistent in collecting feedback so this team habit gets established before you need it to effectively address a critical issue. If it's not, then small issues can quickly spiral out of control.

156

Establish a cadence for your communication so people know what they can expect from you and when. Then schedule time in your personal calendar to make sure you create short, impactful summaries and checklists that leaders find valuable.

157

Make virtual meetings more relationship oriented. Be the "greeter" as people join video conferences. Engage them using chat. Be the "summarizer" to ensure everyone's on the same page. Act as the question-asker, sparking useful dialog.

158

Become a power user for your company's virtual teamwork tools to make your meetings stand out due to their efficiency and effectiveness, and help newbies get up to speed so they can actively participate as soon as possible.

159

Utilize a CRM tool to organize your growing professional network and schedule routine check-ins to share valuable information. Nothing makes you stand out like a post-project check-in that could lead to new opportunities to contribute.

_____

_____

160

Build your "brand" as the person that brings people together, gets work done, and can do it from anywhere, and you'll have tons of LEVERAGE as the company launches new partnerships and looks for leaders to make it happen.

_____

_____

Appendix

1. Check out these free 30 1-minute videos from Kimberly Wiefling on everything from why it's important to stay positive to how to work effectively with people around the world:
https://wiefling.com/resources-tools/1-minute-scrappy-wisdom-videos/.

2. Enjoy these 36 articles and associated 5-minute videos from Kimberly Wiefling, previously published in Japan, for free here:
https://wiefling.com/resources-tools/ask-kimberly-videos-columns/

3. Project Connections has published dozens of articles by Kimberly Wiefling related to project management, and they are available for free here:
https://projectconnections.com/articles/wiefling.html

Contributors

Name of Contributor	
Russell L. Brand https://www.linkedin.com/in/russell-brand/	Chapter 1
Mitchell Levy https://www.linkedin.com/in/mitchelllevy/	Chapter 2
Carole Amos https://www.linkedin.com/in/carole/	Chapter 3
Hong Nguyen-Phuong https://www.linkedin.com/in/hongnguyenp/	Chapter 4
Ellen Grace Henson https://www.linkedin.com/in/ellengracehenson/	Chapter 5
Marcia Daszko https://www.linkedin.com/in/marciadaszko/	Chapter 6
Oliver Yu https://www.linkedin.com/in/oliver-yu-46b97372/	Chapter 7
Susan G. Schwartz https://www.linkedin.com/in/susangschwartz/	Chapter 8
Matthew Cahill https://www.linkedin.com/in/matthewjcahill/	Chapter 9
Camille Smith https://www.linkedin.com/in/camille-smith-a950284/	Chapter 10
Amit Patel https://www.linkedin.com/in/amitpatelstrategyocm/	Chapter 11
Tom Okada https://www.linkedin.com/in/tom-okada-16044a/	Chapter 12
Patricia Corcoran https://www.linkedin.com/in/patriciacorcoranpmp/	Chapter 13
Kimberly Wiefling https://www.linkedin.com/in/scrappykimberlywiefling/	Chapter 14
Annie Sheehan https://www.linkedin.com/in/annie-c-sheehan/	Chapter 15
Jeff Richardson https://www.linkedin.com/in/richardsonjeff/	Chapter 16

Turning Ideas Into Impact

Poet Laureate Stewart Levine's Bio

Stewart Levine is the founder of ResolutionWorks. He is a "resolutionary," counselor, mediator, facilitator, trainer, and author and is widely recognized for creating agreement and empowerment in the most challenging circumstances. He improves productivity while saving the enormous cost of conflict. His innovative work with "Agreements for Results" and his Resolutionary conversational models are unique. As a practicing lawyer, Stewart realized that fighting was an ineffective way of resolving problems. As a marketing executive for AT&T, he saw that the reason collaborations fall apart is that people do not spend time at the beginning of a new working relationship to create clarity about what they want to accomplish together and how they will get there. This is true for employment relationships, joint ventures, and all members of any virtual team. His conversational models create Agreements for Results and a quick return to productivity when working relationships break down. His models for problem solving, collaboration, and conflict resolution are used in many Fortune 100 organizations and have been endorsed by countless thought leaders, including the House Judiciary Committee, 3M, American Express, Chevron, Con-Agra, EDS, General Motors, Harvard Law School, Oracle, Safeco, University of San Francisco, US Department of Agriculture, US Navy, and many others. Stewart teaches communication and conflict management skills for the American Management Association (AMA), CEO Space, and the International Partnering Institute. He is a lecturer at the University of California Berkeley Law School and in the MBA program at Dominican University of California. He was recently inducted into the College of Law Practice Management. Since his content is universal, Stewart speaks before many industry groups, government agencies, and non-profits in a variety of formats, from keynotes to multi-day experiential learning programs and leadership retreats.

More About the Executive Editor

Kimberly Wiefling has been consulting in Silicon Valley and globally for the past 20 years through Wiefling Consulting, and more recently with her team at Silicon Valley Alliances. She's the executive editor of six books in her "Scrappy Guides" series, and the author of Scrappy Project Management, as well as several ThinkAHA books, including Inspired Organizational Cultures. A scientist by education, Kimberly has an MS. in physics and a BS. in chemistry and physics. She worked in HP's analytical products group for nearly a decade, supporting complex systems involving hardware, software, high vacuum, high pressures, gases, liquids, and chemistry called GCMS/LCMS (mass spectrometers). Her roles included on-site customer service/instrument repair, manufacturing engineering, R&D product development program management and quality engineering. She earned her certificate in program and project management through UC Santa Cruz—Silicon Valley where she then taught program and project leadership and management for six years. After more than 100 business trips to Japan and elsewhere globally in the past decade, she's delighted to be working closer to home most of the time—driving to work instead of flying! Kimberly strongly believes that companies doing business across borders and boundaries of every kind are a powerful force for peace in Our World. She is committed to supporting purpose-driven organizations in attracting high-quality investors and the best people through the competitive advantage of a healthy organizational culture. Her big dream is that, one day, both investments and workers will preferentially flow to these kinds of organizations instead of the soul-sucking variety, and the sick, twisted, dysfunctional organizations of Our World will wither and die for lack of financial resources and the talented people they've driven away to more life-affirming workplaces . . . for a better world.

https://kimberlywiefling.com/
https://wiefling.com/
https://siliconvalleyalliances.com/
https://www.amazon.com/Kimberly-Wiefling/e/B002GWKPOG
https://www.amazon.com/Scrappy-Project-Management-Predictable-Avoidable/dp/1600050514/
https://www.amazon.com/Inspired-Organizational-Cultures-Discover-Engage-ebook/dp/B079ZYY4BC/

THiNKaha has created AHAthat for you to share content from this book.

- Share each AHA message socially:
  http://aha.pub/IdeasIntoImpact
- Share additional content: **https://AHAthat.com**
- Info on authoring: **https://AHAthat.com/Author**

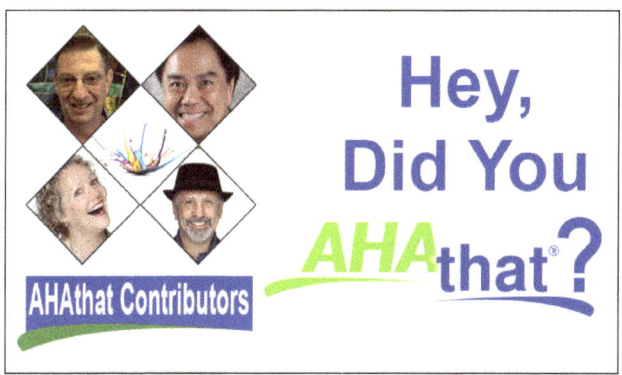

Printed in the USA
CPSIA information can be obtained
at www.ICGtesting.com
JSHW051119041023
49316JS00001B/1